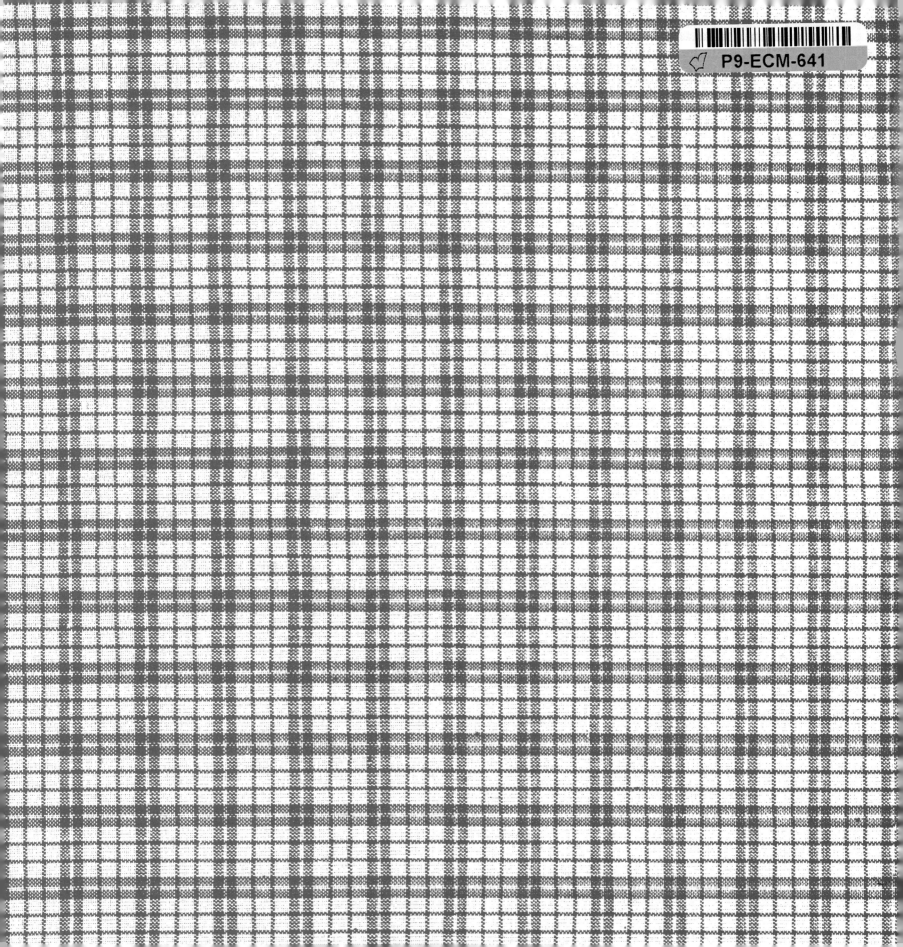

PIERRE DEUX'S
NORMANDY

PIERRE DEUX'S

NORMANDY

A FRENCH COUNTRY STYLE AND SOURCE BOOK

LINDA DANNENBERG,
PIERRE LEVEC,
AND PIERRE MOULIN

Photographs by Guy Bouchet
Design by Paul Hardy

Clarkson N. Potter, Inc./Publishers
DISTRIBUTED BY CROWN PUBLISHERS, INC., NEW YORK

To my father, who has always inspired me—*L.D.*

To Betty Jo and Mary, the keepers of the flame—*P.L.*

To Dominique and Jacques and our mutual
memories of life in wartime Normandy—*P.M.*

Text copyright © 1988 by Linda
Dannenberg, Pierre LeVec, and Pierre
Moulin
Photographs copyright © 1988 by Guy
Bouchet

Published by Clarkson N. Potter, Inc.,
225 Park Avenue South, New York,
New York 10003, and represented in
Canada by the Canadian MANDA
Group.

CLARKSON N. POTTER, POTTER,
and colophon are trademarks of
Clarkson N. Potter, Inc.

Manufactured in Japan

Library of Congress Cataloging-in-
Publication Data
Dannenberg, Linda.
    Pierre Deux's Normandy.
    A French Country Style and Source
Book.
    Includes index.
    1. Decoration and ornament, Rustic
—France—Normandy. 2. Normandy
(France)—Social life and customs.
    I. LeVec, Pierre. II. Moulin, Pierre.
III. Pierre Deux (Firm). IV. Title.
NK1449.A3N65 1988   745.4'49442
88–4079
ISBN 0-517-56079-8
10 9 8 7 6 5 4 3 2 1

First Edition

ACKNOWLEDGMENTS

The enormous pleasure we have had in preparing this book is due in large measure to the people we worked with, dined with, and laughed with over the long course of the project. Some were friends and colleagues of long standing, others we encountered for the first time. Many of these old and new acquaintances, giving variously of their time, their talent, and their expertise, helped in the creation of *Pierre Deux's Normandy*, and we would like to express our appreciation to them here.

Hearty and heartfelt thanks to: David Frost, Anka LeFebvre, Robert Diffenderfer, Barbara Zauft, and David Graham of the Pierre Deux family, New York; our fine agents, Gayle Benderoff and Deborah Geltman; Lydie Marshall of La Bonne Cocotte; George Hern and Marion Fourestier, most helpful liaisons at the French Government Tourist Office; Philippe Pascal, the director of Foods and Wines from France, and his staff; and our mapmaker, Oliver Williams.

Merci infiniment à: Serge Bisono, Isabelle Pilate, et Josephina Bosqued, la famille Pierre Deux à Paris; Marie-Ange Balart, l'amie sage et gentille de Benjamin; Anne d'Ornano, le maire extraordinaire de Deauville; Frédéric Welk de l'Hôtel Normandy, pour son accueil chaleureux; Claude Demais et Odile Hébert, de Calvados Tourisme à Caen; Monsieur Poujhol pour ses bons conseils; Docteur et Madame Claude Levêque; Docteur et Madame Jacques Poilleux; Jenifer et Frédéric Armand-Delille; Martine et Gérard Bazire; Sylvia Étendart; Francine Galiègue et sa famille; Pierre Lafay; Natalie Maintes; Marcel et Marie-Thérèse Le Trésor; Monsieur Liabastre, du Musée du Vieux Honfleur; Étienne Dupont; Étienne Dulin; Simon Chaye; Monsieur Vermughen, le maire de Beuvron-en-Auge; Henri Pennec; et Gérard et Irène Livry-Level, pour un accueil et des repas à rêver.

A very special thanks to Guy Bouchet, our partner and photographer, for his sublime photographs, his lively company, and his patience in circumstances and hours beyond the call of duty.

Thanks also to Paul Hardy, our designer on this book as well as on *French Country*, whose talent and keen imagination set off our words and photographs to such advantage.

Finally, our deepest gratitude goes to our friends at Clarkson N. Potter, Inc., and Crown Publishers, Inc., whose enthusiasm and support from the dawn of our association has been truly inspiring: Alan Mirken, Bruce Harris, Carol Southern, Gael Towey, Ann Cahn, Teresa Nicholas, Jonathan Fox, and of course our sensitive, sympathetic, and superb editor, Nancy Novogrod.

C O N T E N T S

PREFACE

Everyone has two countries, his own and France.
—BENJAMIN FRANKLIN

The allure of France is as powerful as first love and just as ineffable. While the secret of France's seductive spell remains elusive, facets of the mystique are obvious. The beauty and grace of the landscape—so distinctive, so diverse, from Lille near the Belgian border to Perpignan on the southwest Mediterranean coast, from Annécy in the Alpine east to Arcachon on the southern Atlantic coast—are certainly compelling. Also significant is a long and inspiring cultural history cast with an extraordinary assemblage of artists, writers, and statesmen of genius. The cuisine of France, of course, continues to be a potent draw. In a land where each region takes passionate pride in its culinary specialties, a tradition

of great chefs, from George Auguste Escoffier to Joël Robuchon, ensures some of the finest meals in the world. And then there is the awesome richness of the country's architectural style —the mansions of François Mansart and the heroic 18th- and 19th-century public buildings of Paris, the half-timbered *manoirs* and slate-roofed châteaus of Normandy, the thatched-roof cottages of Brittany, the colorful and harmonious Provençal *mas*, or farmhouses, of the Midi, and the gabled houses set on cobbled lanes in Alsace.

But if there is a key to the magic, it has to be in the tiny details and vignettes of daily life: a bistro serving up delicate crepes under flowering apple trees in a hillside Norman village; Parisian mothers meeting their small children at the school steps at four o'clock with bars of chocolate and fresh *baguettes*; the ritual gatherings of old men in the Midi for lazy afternoons of gossip, *pastis*, and a round of *boules*; the carefully grouped pots of cheerful red geraniums on a cottage windowsill in an Alsatian hamlet; the daily race of little fishing boats back to port in southern Brittany; the good-natured haggling over a bright pyramid of carrots at an open market in the Dordogne; the doorway of a half-timbered 17th-century house in Upper Normandy, lushly garlanded

with wisteria. These, as well as countless other scenes and customs, make up the French *art de vivre*, or life-style, that is so appealing.

France, in look, feel, taste, and spirit, is a country like no other. In spite of inevitable modernization—encroaching shopping complexes, parking lots, drugstores, and high-rise office towers—it remains unique. As travel-guide writer Eugene Fodor remarks, "France is still the France of our dreams."

In the series we call *Living in France* we will present individually the great French provinces, beginning in this volume with Normandy. We will travel throughout each region, visiting houses, gazing at the landscapes, learning of the arts and the crafts, and dining on regional cuisine. We will feature homes—from cottage to château—in all their detail, and spotlight some of the families who live within. Our goal is to portray, through our own personal prism, the style, the spirit, the idiosyncrasies, and the romance of each region. For us, this is truly a labor of love.

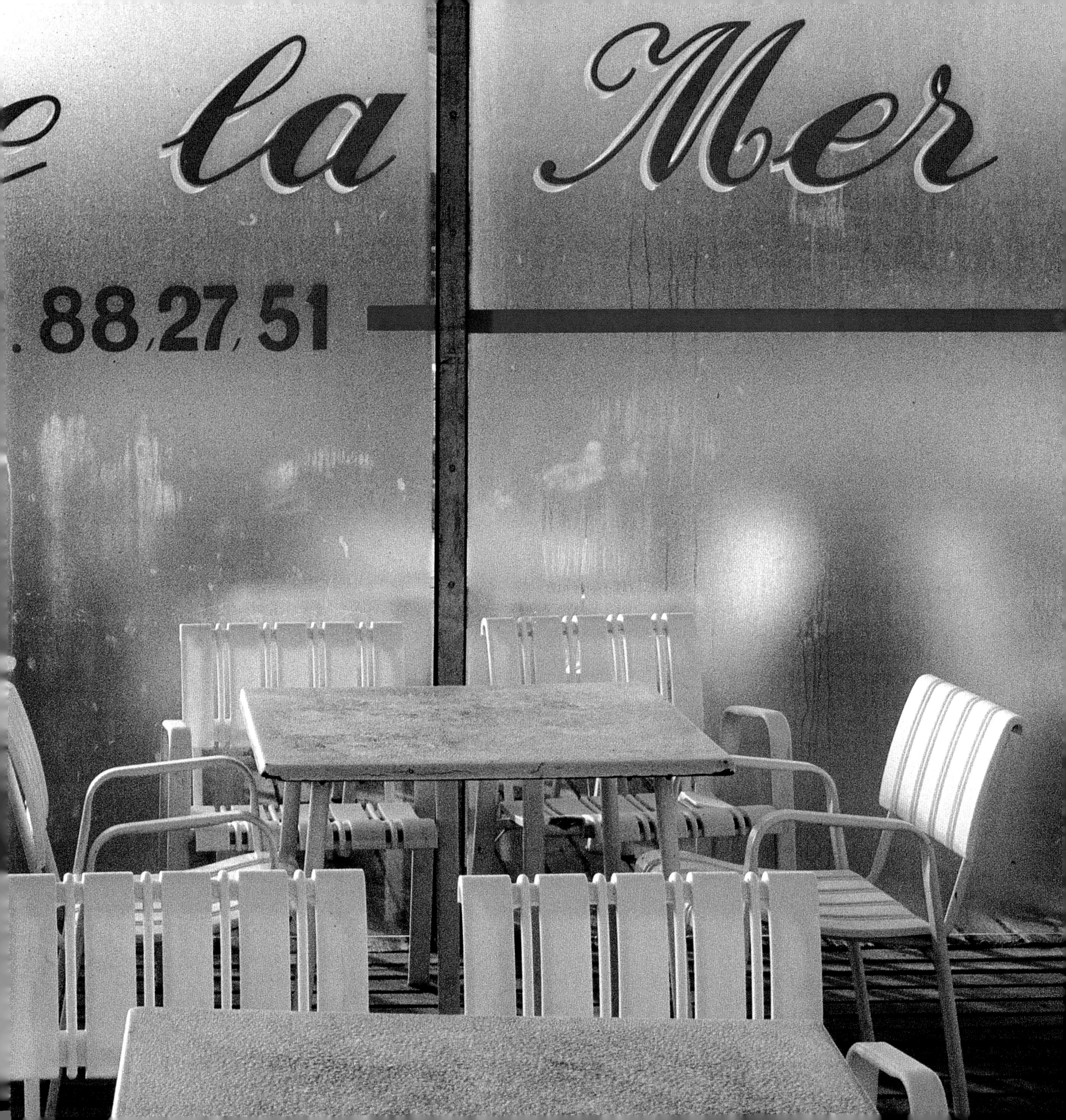
la Mer
.88,27,51

INTRODUCTION

With its sun-stippled country lanes, rolling orchards lush with soft pink apple blossoms, and quaint, half-timbered houses shaded by oaks and willows, Normandy is a soft-focus kind of place. Even assessed *sur place* rather than viewed in the canvases of Boudin, Corot, or Monet, the landscape of this green and graceful province has an impressionistic quality. The perception comes from the way the light filters through the tall old trees; or is diffused over a horse meadow in the early morning haze that lingers until noon; or illuminates the plump cumulus clouds moving across the pastel sky.

Boudin, the pre-impressionist painter called "king of the heavens," was enraptured by the Norman sky near Honfleur. For Courbet it was the interplay of sea and sky over the Seine estuary. Corot was inspired throughout his life by the gentle, poetic beauty of the lush green countryside he knew as a child. And Monet, protégé of Boudin and a member of the artistic band that haunted Honfleur in the mid- to late 1800s, was beguiled by the entire experience of being in Normandy, under the springtime apple blossoms as well as in an early and unusual snow. "Every day I discover ever more beautiful things," he wrote to the painter Frédéric Bazille. "It's enough to drive one mad, so strong is the desire to do everything; my head is reeling!"

The colors of Normandy come straight from the impressionist's palette. The misty greens of the wheat fields in the morning; the creamy white and blush pink, softly blending, of the apple blossoms in the Pays d'Auge; the shimmering golden haze over an orchard in an autumn sunset; the softly mottled blues, mauves, and lavenders that define the Seine estuary as the day grows long; and the pale, iridescent sky overall —these tints and tones create tableaus that enchant on viewing and linger long after in memory.

Rustic and serene, yet only a two- or three-hour drive west from

The Café du Coiffeur, with its array of outdoor tables, occupies one of the many refurbished houses in the restored 16th-century village of Beuvron-en-Auge.

Paris, Normandy has for centuries been the desired vacation spot for wealthy Parisians. Their superb châteaus and *manoirs* peep out through clearings in the greenery all over the province and give an aura of elegance to the countryside.

The hamlets and byways of the Norman hinterland are rich in vistas and country charm of a kind sought by many visitors to France. Take the tiny D22 road south from Honfleur toward Bonneville-la-Louvet and you will pass one of the region's most spectacular fields of flame-red poppies. Drive along the D48 south of Pont l'Évêque and you will come to Pierrefitte-en-Auge, an extraordinary little hamlet of thatched-roof cottages with a rustic bistro—Les Deux Tonneaux—that offers cider, crepes, and other simple fare by a fireplace hung with old copper pots. Worn stone chapels, ivy-covered manor houses, rambling rose gardens, and brick-sided barns are as much a part of the harmonious landscape as the apple trees and the broad, neat, grassy fields.

To live in Normandy, or even to sojourn there for a few days or weeks, is to enjoy a verdant province of remarkable richness. Achingly fertile, the fields produce tons and tons of the best sugar beets, oats, and wheat that abundantly supply the rest of France. Cows nourished by the land provide the milk that becomes the region's voluptuous *crème fraîche*, as well as a multitude of famous cheeses, from Camembert to Pont l'Évêque. The sea that washes the coast from Le Tréport, north of Dieppe, down to Mont-Saint-Michel offers up boatloads of fleshy fish,

Laden with dairy products gathered in her sturdy basket, a shopper returns home from Honfleur's Saturday-morning market.

11

mussels, oysters, and shrimp. But perhaps more than anything else, it is the apple that symbolizes the plenty of this vast, undulating region. The orchards that cover the Pays d'Auge yield Alpine hillocks of red, green, and golden apples, the majority of which are pressed for cider or Calvados, while the rest are either packed for export or are used locally throughout the year for *tarte aux pommes* and a variety of succulent dishes.

The style of Normandy is a rich mix of elegance, earthy functionalism spawned from the region's agricultural heart, and the inspired craftsmanship of Norman stonemasons and carpenters. The province's abundant wood, stone, straw, and slate have been precisely crafted over the centuries by master artisans, creating dwellings as simple as a farm cottage or as graceful, elegant, and harmonious as an aristocratic stone manor house. As for the soaring *flamboyant* gothic cathedrals of Rouen, Caen, and Bayeux, they are in a realm by themselves, in the firmament of architectural masterworks.

The artisans of Normandy, deeply committed to regional traditions but at the same time rather sophisticated in their creative approach, have always been aware of the trends in Paris. The lines of the pretty armoires, chairs, and tables of 18th- and 19th-century Normandy, often sculpted in oak, reflect contemporaneous fashions of the capital, while the elaborate floral carving that adorns the pieces is purely regional.

The skills and traditions of the gifted lacemakers of Alençon and Bayeux have their roots in 17th-century Venice, where the 17th-century minister Jean Baptiste Colbert recruited a group of Italian lacemakers to bring their craft to France. But the Norman *dentellières* soon made the craft their own, turning out exquisite handmade lace that was prized the world over.

After school on Saturday morning, three little girls in the Pays d'Auge carry home their pet rabbit.

Pride in craftsmanship and in perpetuating a venerable tradition is apparent not only among the handful of lacemakers still producing Bayeux and Alençon lace, but also among the artisans of Villedieu-les-Poêles. Using production processes virtually unchanged for centuries, they turn out the magnificent, pitch-perfect church bells of the Fonderie de Cloches, or bell foundry, in one part of town, and world-renowned, hand-hammered copperware in another.

The people of Normandy are traditionally characterized as being stoic, stubborn, and reserved, qualities inherited, along with a taste for adventure and exploration, from their Viking ancestors. These dauntless but dour Norsemen had been invading what came to be called Normandy for more than six hundred years before they officially established themselves in the province in 911, led by their powerful chief, Rolf-le-Marcheur. The Vikings, good farmers as well as good sailors, cultivated the land and developed trade routes that soon made Normandy one of France's most flourishing provinces. By the time Rolf, then called Rollon, died about twenty years later, the Vikings were well assimilated into their French surroundings. But their legacy of fearlessness lived on. William the Conqueror, Samuel de Champlain, and Cavalier de la Salle of Rouen are only a few of the intrepid Normans who carried on the winning ways of their ancestors.

On market day, residents of the small town of Honfleur stock up on fresh vegetables in the Place Sainte-Catherine.

Despite his distinctive ancestral traits of courage and curiosity, *Le Normand* today is generally not an extrovert. You won't find in Normandy the effusive, open-armed welcome you would encounter in a region like Provence. It may take an hour of conversation or a day or two's residence in an *auberge* before you detect a reticent smile from your host and a letting down of the guard.

Normandy demands a slow and gentle acquaintanceship. Like the best friendships, Normandy rewards with repeated encounters, yielding each time a greater understanding and a deeper love.

The elegant brick Château de Martainville, above, built at the end of the 15th century, eight miles east of Rouen, is today a museum of Norman furniture and folk art.

Channel

CHERBOURG
Tourlaville
Cape Lévy
Goury
Barfleur
St-Vaast-la-Hougue
Flamanville
Valognes
le Hoc Point
OMAHA BEACH
Arromanches
Courseulles-sur-M
Bricquebec
Ste-Mère-Eglise
Carteret
Douve
BESSIN
Bayeux
Cabou
CAEN
Lessay
ST. LÔ
CAMPAGN
CAEN
Vire
Coutances
Clécy
BOCAGE
SUISSE NORMANDE
Granville
Villedieu-les-Poêles
Vire
Falai
Sée
Ar
Avranches
Flers
la Ferté
Mont-St-Michel
Sélune
Domfront
Bagnole
de-l'Orn

The

COTENTIN

COUTANGAIS

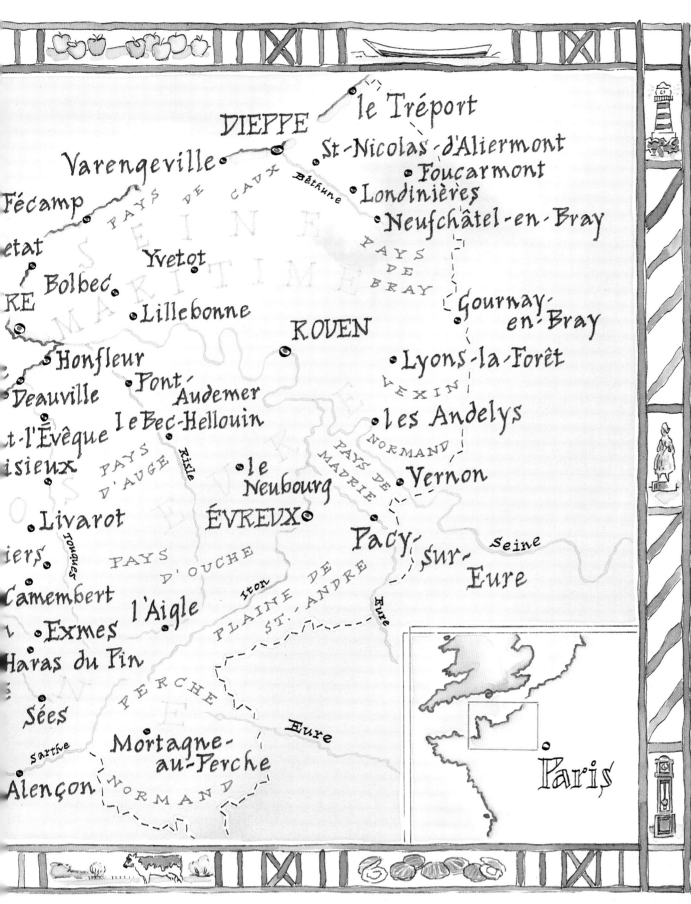

le Tréport

DIEPPE

St-Nicolas-d'Aliermont

Varengeville

Foucarmont

Londinières

Fécamp

etat

Neufchâtel-en-Bray

Bolbec

Yvetot

Lillebonne

Gournay-en-Bray

ROUEN

Honfleur

Lyons-la-Forêt

Deauville

Pont-Audemer

t-l'Évêque

le Bec-Hellouin

les Andelys

isieux

le Neubourg

Vernon

Livarot

ÉVREUX

iers

Pacy-Sur-Eure

Camembert

l'Aigle

Exmes

Haras du Pin

Sées

Mortagne-au-Perche

Alençon

Paris

On the property of the great abbey in Le Bec-Hellouin, above, a twin-spired outbuilding —L'Abbatiale—houses an automobile museum of fifty classic cars.

A PROVINCIAL ALBUM

Normandy is a province of striking contrasts. Twenty minutes away from the smart, sophisticated town of Deauville is the half-timbered country town of Pont l'Évêque and only five minutes farther on is the profoundly rural village of Pierrefitte-en-Auge. The lavish seaside setting of *belle époque* Cabourg quickly yields to the orchards and pastures of the hinterland in nearby Bavent. The lush, primeval hills and gorges of the Suisse Normande could not be more different in spirit and geography from the austere, windswept coast of Cherbourg. ❦ Its intriguing contrasts in textures and moods make Normandy a wonderful place to roam. You never know beyond what twist in a country lane you will see a superb spired and slate-roofed *manoir,* or two thoroughbred stallions, perfect as bookends, nuzzling in the late-afternoon haze. Taking the most obscure "white roads" visible on the map (as opposed to

the larger "yellow" and "red" routes) provides the most satisfying discoveries—a vista above a river canyon to the dense forest beyond; a great château, looming at the other side of a field of oats, with just one light burning at dusk; an enclave of thatched-roof cottages banked by mounds of newly harvested apples. A walk along the Côte d'Albâtre—the chalky cliffs that echo those of Dover across the Channel—might evoke the sensations that inspired painters to introduce the soft brushstrokes of impressionism into their landscapes. Further west, the beaches hold sadder memories

—of the Allied soldiers who fell here on D-Day, 1944. ❡ From the orchards of Victot-Pontfol to the great stud farms east of Alençon, from the broad *planches* of Deauville to the weathered fences of Barneville, herewith an album of the many facets and feelings of Normandy.

IMPRESSIONS OF NORMANDY

The soft and shimmering light that illuminates the Norman landscape, seashore, villages, or city endows the image with a painterly allure as intense as a first viewing of Monet's water lilies. In inclement weather, under steely skies, Normandy takes on a different mood: more somber, more withdrawn, more two-dimensional. In this guise, under a cloak of tone-on-tone grays, the Norman landscape becomes the province of Georges Seurat, who was fascinated by the region's "indefinable grays," and in a series of canvases in the late 1800s evoked the leaden clouds and lonely quays of Honfleur with his signature tiny brushstrokes.

The town of Le Bec-Hellouin, left, sits snugly in the placid countryside of the Risle Valley on a crisp early fall morning. Through half-closed eyes, the scenery along a country lane near Honfleur, right, resembles an impressionist's canvas. On the following pages are some scenes from Normandy life.

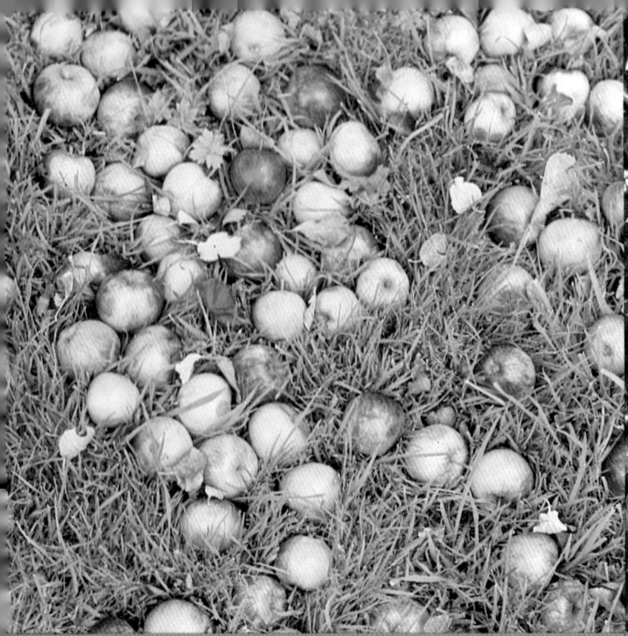
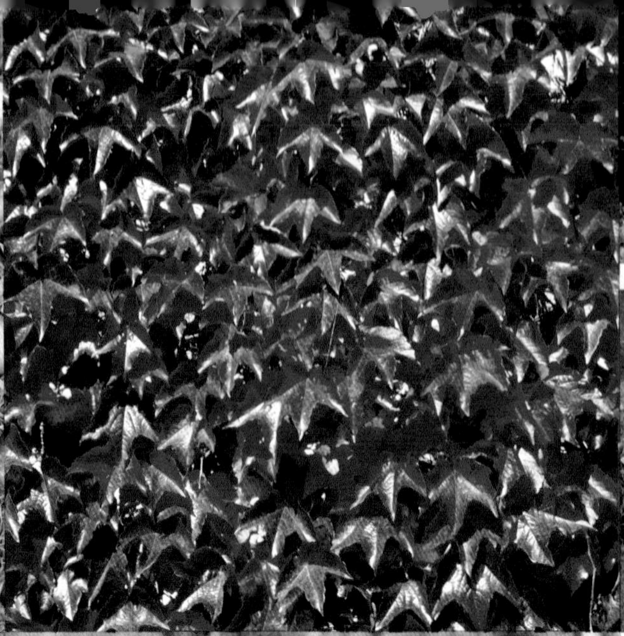
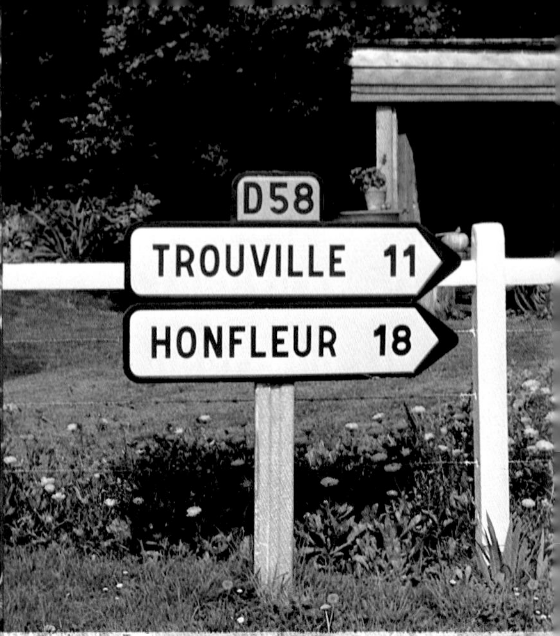
D58
TROUVILLE 11
HONFLEUR 18
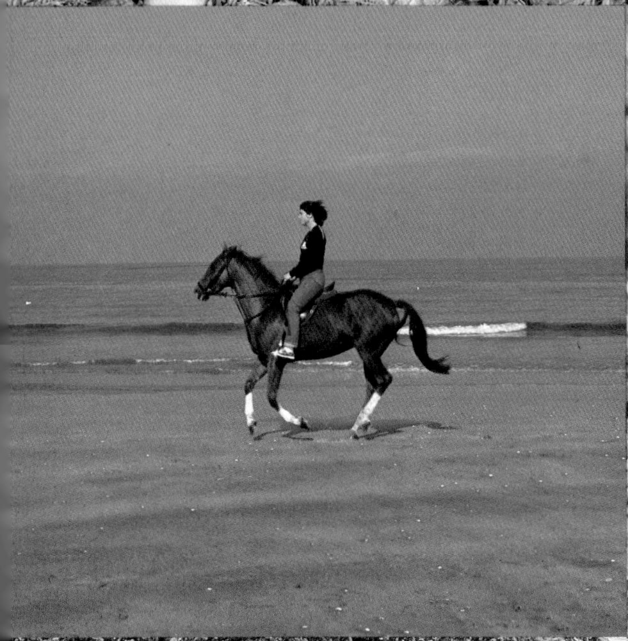
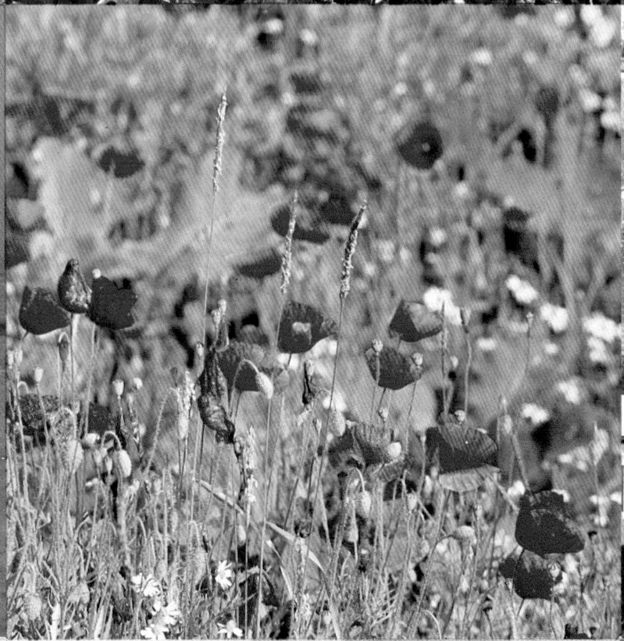
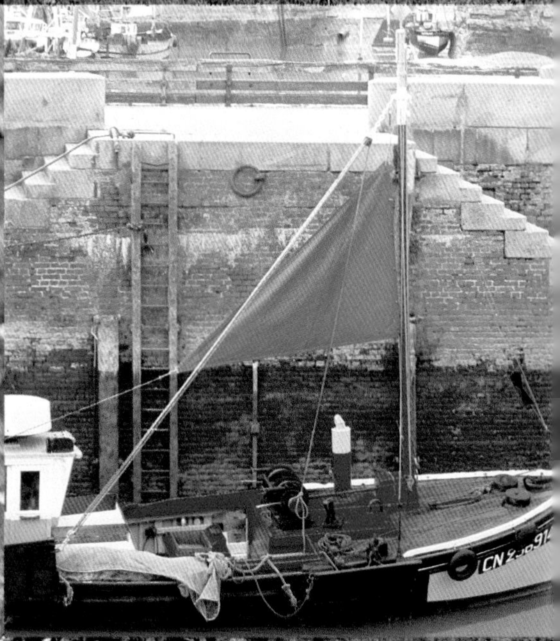
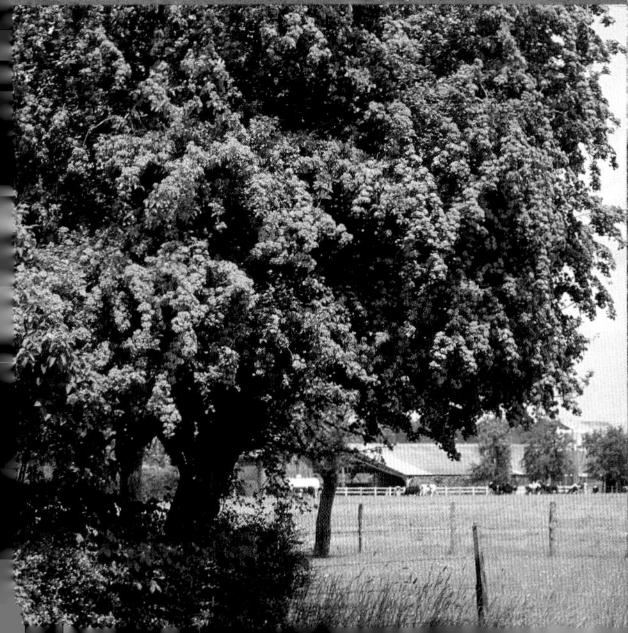
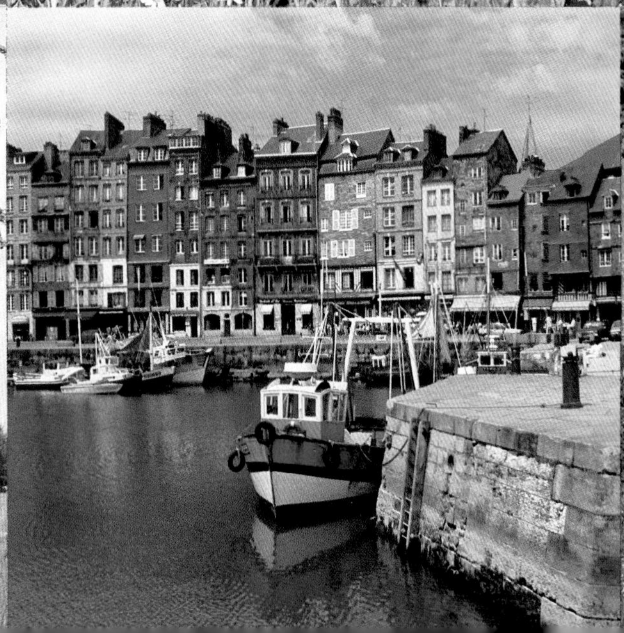
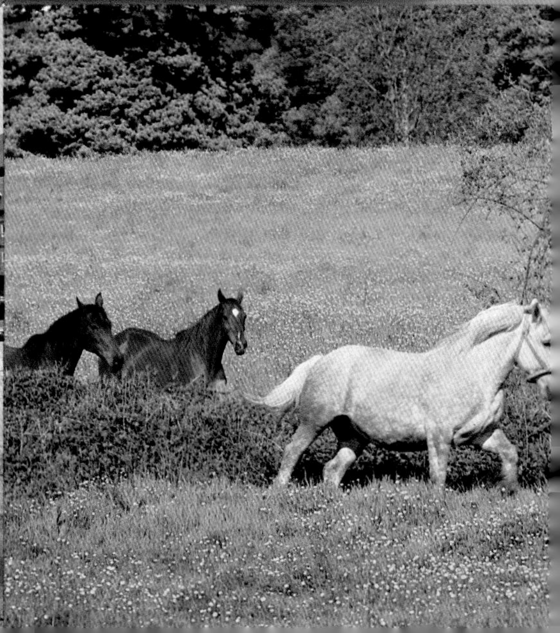

Mont Saint-Michel, France's most majestic landmark, marks the coastal boundary between Normandy and Brittany, right. For centuries both provinces have laid claim to this tiny granite island, topped by the incomparable Saint-Michel abbey, a phenomenon of architectural ingenuity and skill created between the 11th and 16th centuries. Every granite block, brought in from Brittany or the Chausey Islands of Normandy, had to be hoisted up 263 feet to the peak. Until a causeway was built in the 1960s, Mont Saint-Michel was accessible only at low tide; high tide inundated the one road with lightning speed and was often a lethal surprise to unwary travelers. Today, the Mont has a population of a little over one hundred residents, although hundreds of thousands of visitors flock to the site each year.

In early evening, fog rises from the gently flowing Charentonne River, far left. A delightfully detailed house, left, overlooks the fields of Saint Martin-aux-Chartrains. A carpet of delicate white flowers covers the forest floor of a vast estate near Lisieux, below far left. A handsome manor house is almost obscured by morning mist, below left. Under a leafy canopy, a rural lane, right, leads to a farm deep in the countryside.

APPLE COUNTRY

The delicate scent of apple blossoms in the spring, the pungent, earthy smell of apples stored in an old barn awaiting the press in the fall—these two glorious fragrances sensuously evoke the experience of being in Normandy more profoundly than anything else could. Normandy is apple country, first and foremost. The ranks of sturdy, gently gnarled apple trees stretching over gently swelling hills form the region's most characteristic landscape.

Apple-blossom time classically lasts four lovely weeks, from mid-April to mid-May. Harvesttime spans the fall, from September, when the early eating apples from the Bocage region south of Saint-Lô are ready, to early December, when the hard, crisp apples of the Auge region are ripe for picking.

The pure, sweet juice of the apples, which bear quaint varietal names such as "Tranquil" and "Fieldmouse Red," becomes either *cidre bouché,* a sparkling fermented cider sold in a cork-topped bottle—the popular accompaniment to the local seafood, chicken, or lamb—or Calvados, the potent apple brandy (or applejack) for which the region is justly famed. *"Un Calva," très vieux* or *hors d'âge,* is the *digestif* of choice to cap a night in Normandy. And then, of course, there is the famous *trou Normand.* This is a small glass of Calvados downed between courses of a rich Norman meal to make a *trou,* or hole—that is, more space for subsequent courses. Whether as pure juice, sparkling cider, or Calvados, the nectar of the apples is Normandy's water of life.

Cows in an apple orchard in full blossom are a common sight in the Normandy countryside, left. The cows here are Holsteins, however, not a breed usually found in Normandy, where the native cows have straight backs and black "eyeglasses." Undulating hillocks of apples, right, are a common fall sight in Calvados country.

At the end of a day of harvesting, a farm-hand, above, pulls away from the apple barn on the property of Étienne Dupont.

A just-plucked apple is a picture of perfection, above. Burlap sacks of harvested apples, right, await the tractor-drawn wagon in the Dupont orchards.

Neither words nor pictures can convey the intoxicating aroma of fresh apples and old wood in a *grenier à pommes,* or apple storehouse, right, just after the harvest. Nineteenth-century Calvados casks are stored in a small barn, below right, on the Saint Martin-aux-Chartrains property of Joseph Debreuil, another top Calvados producer.

LE HARAS DU PIN

Behind a tall, elaborate iron gate topped by a gilded horse's head lies France's premier national stud farm, the Haras du Pin. Here, just east of Argentan, in a sublime setting of aristocratic grace and tranquillity, lithe-limbed thoroughbreds, born to race, as well as awesome white Percheron workhorses of mythological proportions, are bred and raised.

The Haras du Pin was established in 1715 and opened to the first horses, after fifteen years of construction, in 1730. Designed by Jules Hardouin-Mansart and landscaped by André Lenôtre, it was one of several *haras* built after Louis XIV's minister Colbert instituted the concept of state-sponsored horse-breeding farms in 1665. Originally created to breed cavalry horses for the king's army, and later workhorses for the region's farms, the Haras today devotes most of its reasonably priced stud services to breeding horses destined for the racetrack.

The pale, elegant 18th-century château of gray slate and white stone looks out over a wide horseshoe-shaped courtyard flanked by stables of rosy brick. Called the Horse's Versailles, the Haras du Pin lodges its 300 equine guests in unrivaled elegance: 18th-century stables quoined with Caen limestone and designed with vaulted doorways and mullioned windows. The grounds, covering more than 27,000 acres of woods, fields, trails, and tracks, are shaded by towering ancient oaks. A specialized school, the École Nationale des Haras, is also on the grounds of Le Pin to train the future staffs of France's twenty-two national stud farms.

The graceful 18th-century château of the Haras du Pin, designed by Hardouin-Mansart and landscaped by Lenôtre, dominates the landscape east of Argentan.

The château is rich in striking architectural details, such as this terra-cotta tiled roof, below left, set with dormer windows, over the brick-walled stable.

The brilliant red *H,* below center, is a symbol of France's national stud farm.

Some of the personnel from this premier national stud smile down from the steps of the stable enclave, below right. The symmetrical and elegantly designed stables, bottom left, are kept as pristinely as the more formal parts of the property. One of the massive Percherons bred at the Haras du Pin, the 1,700-pound Kleber, takes a joyous leap during his afternoon exercise, bottom right.

Closely resembling the pattern of a Hermès tie, harnesses in the tack room, below left, are neatly displayed against a vibrant blue background. Several of Le Pin's prize Percherons, below right, graze in the pastures that stretch out from the château. A sleek and elegant slate cupola topped with a very appropriate weather vane, bottom left, adorns a stable roof. Remarkable workmanship distinguishes even a polished brass water spigot, bottom center, on a stable wall. A wide arched doorway, bottom right, leads into the 18th-century stable, or *écurie*.

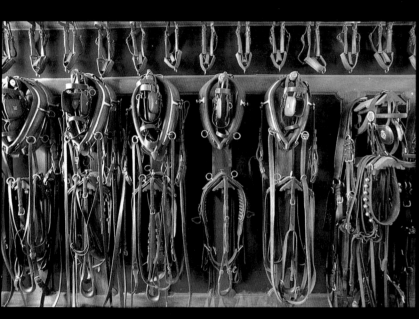

In the stone-paved vestibule of the Château du Pin, right, an equestrian decor includes a hunting horn, 19th-century engravings of horses, an antique rifle, a studsman's cap, and a riding crop.

A Le Pin studsman shows off Floreston, the Haras's prize purebred black stallion, right. Medals and awards for venerable champions originating at the Haras du Pin proudly grace the walls of a stable office, far right. Kept in prime condition, pieces of Le Pin tack, below right, gleam on their pegs. The Haras carriage, driven by one of the studsmen, with another as passenger, sets out on a sunny afternoon, below far right.

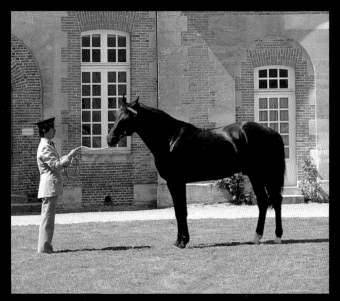

A courtyard of the Hotel Normandy, right, shelters both lawn furniture and the vintage automobile parked by a weekend guest.

TRS 901

DEAUVILLE

In France, the name Deauville conjures up the image of slim, elegant women strolling the boardwalk, one hand holding a parasol, the other restraining a tiny dog at the end of a leash. The parasols are gone now, as are this resort's glory years of the twenties and thirties; the little dogs, ever present, have diminished in number. But Deauville perseveres, an immaculate town carefully planted with arrangements of seasonal flowers throughout the year. Set on the edge of a vast and extraordinary beach popular for horseback riding at dawn or dusk, Deauville still has great cachet as a luxurious international resort and continues to draw a wealthy, sophisticated clientele.

Much of the town's attraction has to do with money and horses. Deauville's spectacular casino, with its glamorous private salon for high rollers, is renowned. Gambling knows no season; you can wager your money any day of the year in the gaming rooms of Deauville. But for the horsey set the time for Deauville is August, a month of races and polo matches, capped at the end by the Deauville Grand Prix and the yearling sales.

Two legendary hotels, both fronting the sea, welcome guests who happen to be deprived of villas of their own in town: the grand, distinctive Normandy, a gabled, half-timbered, mossy green work of fantasy, and her rival sister, the more classic,

A busboy, above right, sets up floral centerpieces before Sunday luncheon in the garden. Classic cars are gathered for an annual antique auto weekend at the Hotel Normandy, right.

glittering Royale. Set on the small streets between the two hotels, like so many fashionable jewels, are tiny, supremely chic outposts of such shops as Hermès, Cartier, and Au Printemps. These and other intriguing boutiques beckon irresistibly to strollers out for a late-afternoon walk before cocktails at the Normandy's cozy piano bar or at the Royale.

Across the broad Boulevard Eugène Cornuché, stretching along the beach, are clusters of cabanas, bars, and restaurants, such as the Bar du Soleil and Le Ciro's, and, of course, *les planches,* Deauville's wide, weathered boardwalk. Dotting the beach in season, to the point where their colors merge into an impressionistic sea, are the famous bright red, blue, and orange beach umbrellas and tents, spread wide to shelter the tan and glistening bodies of the summer *Deauvillais.* At least once a day, if not twice, one must make a sortie back and forth across the *planches* to see, to be seen, and to check out the newest arrivals at the Bar du Soleil. Deauville in season couldn't be more fashionable or more French.

Handsome toile de Jouy fabric on a seat, above, adds elegance to the large, dazzling theater of the Casino de Deauville, right.

Two large Art Deco murals, above, painted in 1928, dominate the comfortable bar across from the casino's gaming rooms.

Furled beach parasols, left, form a colorful battalion along the Deauville beach. A rider sets out over the sands, above. Overleaf: A group of horseback riders stretching across the beach near the water's edge at sunset is one of the scenes most emblematic of Deauville. The vignettes are from Deauville's celebrated boardwalk.

43

The *tricolore*, or French flag, blows in a soft breeze in front of the Mairie de Deauville, the town hall, right.

Anne d'Ornano, seated in front of the *mairie,* above, is Deauville's elegant and dynamic mayor.

The flowers in the pretty gardens of the *mairie,* right, are changed four times a year, with the seasons.

The Villa Strassburger, right, designed by a Caen architect named Pichereau, is described in a landmark commission report as "the most characteristic of Deauville's *belle époque* villas." Lavish architectural details, above, below, and inset, include several levels of dormer windows, turrets, balconies, overhangs, and false timbering.

THE AMERICAN MILITARY CEMETERY

Hard by the landing beaches of the Allied invasion, in the town of Saint-Laurent-sur-Mer, lies the American Military Cemetery—so silent, so majestic, so sad. This emotionally stunning, unforgettable memorial to the soldiers who died in June 1944, in the largest amphibious troop landing in history, covers 172 pristine but somber acres. Even those born after World War II walk away with a knot in their throats after seeing the sea of almost 10,000 small white marble crosses and stars stretching to infinity above Omaha Beach.

The Spirit of American Youth, below, a 22-foot statue created by sculptor Donald De Lue of New York, is inscribed around its base with the words, ''Mine Eyes Have Seen the Glory of the Coming of the Lord.''

Overlooking Omaha Beach, 9,386 headstones mark the graves of soldiers who fell in the Battle of Normandy; 14,000 more soldiers who were originally buried here were later returned home. The cemetery, completed and dedicated in 1956, is maintained by the American Battle Monuments Commission, left. An orientation table set on an overlook parapet, inset right, indicates the landing beaches.

NORMANDY'S GENTLE ANIMAL KINGDOM

In a land spread with farms, pasturelands, and paddocks, it is the animals, the hearty, placid local fauna, who seem to give the region its raison d'être. The sleekly contented *vaches normandes*, distinctive for their white, cream, and dark brown markings and brown-patch "spectacles," are characteristic of the province. And with a representation of more than 6 million head in the region, they are France's dominant breed. Their rich milk —4½ to 6½ gallons a day per cow—provides the cream used to produce the area's golden butter, thick *crème fraîche*, and prized cheeses.

Sheep, chickens, roosters, rabbits, rams, dogs, cats, and superb thoroughbred horses are everywhere, at every turn in Normandy. Very few families, whatever the size of their *domaines*, are without at least one animal—because living in Normandy without animals is not really living in Normandy.

Two thoroughbreds, left, keep company on a hilltop in the Pays d'Auge. Portraits of Normandy's creatures great and small form a lively mosaic, right.

Mignon, Étienne Du-
pont's friendly family
bull, a classic *taureau
normand,* enjoys a
warm fall day in Victot-
Pontfol, right.

LE BEC-HELLOUIN

Even to many who know Normandy well, Le Bec-Hellouin comes as a surprise. This tiny village, set in the Risle Valley twenty-seven miles southwest of Rouen, or about an hour's drive on back roads southeast from Deauville, is almost miragelike in its tranquillity. Strolling the small, empty streets between the half-timbered houses decked with geraniums, one is enveloped by an overwhelming sense of peace. Is this heaven? Perhaps not, but it is the setting for the majestic Benedictine abbey, Notre Dame du Bec-Hellouin, that is the village's main draw.

A visit to this serenely beautiful enclave, where white-robed monks and snowy swans glide by with equal silence and grace, would enrich any excursion through Normandy. Established in the 11th century by a nobleman named Herluin, or Hellouin, who opted for God's service in mid-life, the abbey has been built, destroyed, and rebuilt many times over nine hundred years. The most recent restoration was in 1948.

The peaceful tree-shaded streets of Le Bec-Hellouin, a village in the Risle Valley, are lined with tidy half-timbered houses, left; in the background is the 15th-century Tour Saint-Nicolas. A white-robed monk offers a sympathetic ear at the abbey of Notre Dame du Bec-Hellouin, right.

A Benedictine monk,
above, sits with a visi-
tor among the stones of
the medieval abbey.

The vast property of
Notre Dame du Bec-
Hellouin, left, which in-
cludes a 15th-century
tower, the remains of a
medieval abbey, and
an automobile mu-
seum, dominates the
village of Le Bec-
Hellouin.

An ancient sarcophagus rests undisturbed under a coating of moss, left, outside the walls of the chapel. A placid *rivière* flows through the abbey's property, right.

WINTER SCENES

Snow is rare in Normandy. With its generally mild, temperate climate, Normandy enjoys winter temperatures that average 43° F. Fog and rain, and a luminous, hazy overcast, are the norm in Normandy, interspersed with dazzling clear and dry periods that can last for days. But snow is the startling exception, and when it falls it's occasion enough to capture the event for posterity, as Monet did in *La Charrette. Route sous la neige à Honfleur (The Cart. Snow-covered Road Near Honfleur)*. One early winter day we came upon Normandy in the snow and we found the land transformed into a crystalline kingdom of dreams.

On the morning after a rare snowfall, a lone cow, far right, attempts to graze on frozen grasses. A thick blanket of snow hides the thatched roof of a small barn, right, softens the spikes of a château's wrought-iron fence, above, and gives a cherubic statue a frosty *chapeau,* left.

ROUEN AT CHRISTMAS

One of France's tragic, martyred cities, burned in 1940 and bombed in 1944, Rouen has restored and reconstructed its great cathedrals, monuments, and ports over the last four decades, a massive, daunting undertaking. Today Rouen, the capital of Upper Normandy (Caen is the region's other capital, representing Lower Normandy), is a lively modern city with an extraordinary old quarter, delightful for browsing, strolling, and antiquing. Shadowing the winding, narrow streets of Le Vieux Rouen are more than 700 half-timbered houses dating from the Middle Ages to the end of the 1700s. Many antiques shops occupy the first-floor commercial spaces, interspersed among a variety of restaurants and cafés, from inexpensive bistros to Michelin-starred establishments. Symbolic of the old quarter, and of Rouen itself, is the Gros-Horloge, the colossal and ornate clock that tops the archway leading to the Place du Vieux-Marché, the old covered marketplace.

Here is Rouen at Christmas, a time when the city discreetly decks itself in an understated display of contemporary lighting and the shops fill with an abundance of holiday treats—foie gras; *boudin blanc*, the mild white sausage traditional on Christmas eve; and the elaborate Yule log cake, the *bûche de Noël*.

The streets and shop windows of Rouen, left, are festive with the adornments and delicacies of the season. A jolly Saint Nick, right, obscures the timbers above a shop in Rouen's old quarter.

THE STYLE OF NORMANDY

An exceptional craftsmanship distinguishes the architecture and artisanal work of Normandy. The patient, intricate efforts required to create the sought-after laces of Alençon and Bayeux are well documented. But the construction of a brick barn or a columnar dovecote in complex patterns of brick, stone, mortar, and wood is no less demanding, and involves an artistry and commitment all its own. A small buttressed and timbered *manoir* balcony, a massive yet gracefully sculpted 16th-century handrail, and a striking 17th-century church built by local chandlers are especially impressive examples of the masterly use of wood. Descendants of the Norsemen, the Normans have perpetuated the skills of their Viking ancestors, who were shipbuilders and carpenters *extraordinaire*. ❡ *Le style normand* is an intriguing and gracefully appealing blend of naiveté and a touch of sophistication. It is

provincial, of course, shaped, like all traditional country styles, by necessity, function, and climate, yet in Normandy there has always been an awareness of *la mode* up the river in Paris. You might see a sleek Mansart-inspired roof similar to one on a Parisian town house topping a typically Norman half-timbered facade, or a fireplace with Louis XV lines as the centerpiece of the living room of a rambling 18th-century farmhouse in the Pays d'Auge. Armoires, chairs, buffets, and clocks also display both rustic and formal qualities. ❡ Despite outside influences from the capital and abroad, *le style normand* remains at heart profoundly re-

gional. Furniture, crafts, and all manner of decorative elements from Normandy are among the finest examples of *art populaire* in France. It is in Normandy that people have clung most tenaciously to their traditions, restoring, where necessary, with love and care.

THE NORMAN HOUSE: OUTSIDE

A remarkable diversity of materials makes up the **facades** of Norman dwellings. There are half-timbered houses of heavy oak beams and plaster; houses of slate, brick, limestone, flint, or shale; houses of granite, and houses that combine four or even five different materials in one intricate facade. This broad range of styles is testimony to the great imagination and technical expertise of Normandy's master builders.

The most characteristic and traditional Norman structure, however, is the half-timbered house or barn of Upper Normandy—the eastern part of the province. Usually called *colombage* or *pan de bois*, both denoting wood-ribbed construction, the half-timbered style has its roots in the Middle Ages. By the Renaissance, the style had been abandoned in other provinces, but it persisted in Normandy well into the 19th century, despite newer, more practical, and more economical styles. *Le Normand* was simply happier and more comfortable surrounded by his rustic beams.

The heavy exposed timbers of these classic Norman homes are separated by a variety of fillings. Some simple dwellings are filled with *bauge,* a malleable mixture of clay and straw, while others

A flower box of cheerful geraniums, left, is a traditional accent on the *chaumières*, or thatched-roof cottages, in Calvados, as well as on the stone-bordered windowsills of grander dwellings, such as the 17th-century château in the Pays d'Auge, right.

are finished with plaster. For more elaborate structures, patterned brickwork, or thin tiles of terracotta called *tuileaux*, or even *silex* (flint) set in mortar, may be used between the timbers. The beams themselves are worked in a range of patterns, from narrow, vertical, columnar arrangements to intricate, crosshatched, "woven," or even latticework designs. Occasionally, a whole tree trunk with branches intact will serve as the main vertical and horizontal beams, creating *colombage* facades that are sturdy and beautiful, but do require frequent maintenance.

Stone houses fashioned in roughly hewn granite or limestone are the dwellings most traditional in Lower Normandy, the western part of the province, which includes the Cotentin peninsula down to Mont-Saint-Michel. Solid almost to the point of being indestructible, these stone houses have admirably stood the test of time. Dotting the landscape are many fine examples of these farmhouses and *manoirs*, built along strong horizontal lines and dating from the 16th and 17th centuries. Very different in mood and spirit from the charming half-timbered houses to the east, the stone residences, with their rigorous geometric silhouettes, communicate an austere and indomitable strength.

The typical Norman **roofline** is steeply pitched to facilitate good drainage of the frequent rains. The most charming and rustic of regional roofs is the *chaumière*, or straw thatch, usually seen on one-story houses or barns. Once the most economical roofing, the *chaumière* today is the most expensive to achieve, requiring many man-hours of specialized labor. Nevertheless, the traditional thatched roof often crowns restored and even newly constructed

The distinctive walls of the Manoir du Champs Versant, a working farm and bed-and-breakfast in the village of Bonnebosq, are a striking juxtaposition of timbers and geometrically patterned brick and stone, right.

74

buildings. The most classical *chaumières* are adorned with irises planted in a bed of clay along the roof's peak.

Another very typical roof throughout Normandy is constructed of small thin sheets of slate, or *ardoise*, a material that has been used since the 16th century but has grown enormously in popularity over the last two centuries. Lighter and more durable than the terra-cotta tiles it has all but supplanted, the slate roof is also more efficient under the rains, quickly draining the frequent downpours. There are some houses in the Pays d'Auge, notably in and around Honfleur, where slate has been used on the exterior facade as well as on the roof, resulting in a very homogeneous, if somewhat foreboding, aspect.

Terra-cotta roof tiles still dominate the Orne region, Normandy's south, and remain quite well represented throughout Calvados. Occasionally, on a grand manor house, glazed tiles are interspersed with the traditional unglazed variety to catch the light and add color and interest to a wide expanse of roof. Rare now in Normandy, but not yet extinct, is the wood-shingled roof, usually laid out in patterns of square and scalloped shingles. Decorating the peaks and corners of the region's tile roofs are imaginative ceramic *faîtages*, colorful figures and forms, which we feature on pages 112–115.

A small cottage in the countryside between the towns of Pont l'Évêque and Deauville, left, is charmingly detailed with fleurs-de-lis and other royal emblems, a shingled roof, and an unusual pattern of timbers. A potpourri of regional design elements, right, such as dormer windows and geometric shingling, adorns houses humble and grand in the Pays d'Auge.

Windows in Normandy, given the region's temperate climate, are among the most generously proportioned of those in all of the French provinces. Tall French windows, opening inward, are often mullioned—made up of small panes of glass divided by wood frames. Some grand antique manor houses have diamond-paned leaded windows protected by heavy wrought-iron grilles. Other venerable dwellings from the 16th or 17th centuries are illuminated by windows that are very small and square. The windows of stone houses are usually symmetrically placed and regularly spaced. The windows of half-timbered structures, however, can be quite irregular and asymmetrical, piercing the facade in odd places. The dormer window is typical throughout Normandy, jutting out of the roof from under a cap of *chaume* as frequently as from under one of slate or terra-cotta tile. These little windows were designed principally to let just a bit of light and air into the attic, where fodder was stored during the winter, both as animal feed and as insulation against the cold.

Archways buttressed with granite blocks sometimes frame the **doorways** of the stone manor houses of the Cotentin, while the doors themselves are often set with mullioned glass. In Upper Normandy doors are small and rectangular, occasionally constructed in two halves, which can open separately —a top half usually with mullioned or leaded-glass windows and a lower half that is solid. A fanlight or transom window is set in above many doorways to illuminate the interior hallway. The entrance doors of some of the region's beautiful châteaus are massive, carved, and sometimes adorned with iron studs. But this look is less representative of Norman style than it is of a pervasive aristocratic taste that knows no province.

The symmetry of this fine 17th-century château, of rosy brick quoined with white limestone, characterizes aristocratic homes built in Upper Normandy in the 1600s, left.

The ivy covering the exterior walls of many Norman houses changes from deep green to scarlet with the coming of autumn. The turn-of-the-century residence, left, along the Normandy Corniche, on the road from Trouville to Honfleur, was photographed in early June; the 19th-century brick residence en route to Cambremer, below left, in October.

At dusk, soft incandescent light pours out of the windows of the Moulin du Vey, left, a stone inn deep in the Suisse Normande, once a working mill.

THE NORMAN HOUSE: INSIDE

No two houses built before the mid-1800s are exactly the same. The Norman was too much of an individualist, and prided himself on the originality of his home. There are, however, some common features in many Norman homes of a certain standing, seen throughout the region.

The traditional Norman **floor** is made from terracotta tile. By using a variety of shades, shapes, and sizes of tile, the builder of each home could differentiate its floor from its neighbor's. Called *pavé*, the tiles may be hexagonal, square, or rectangular. They are extremely durable and easy to maintain; centuries-old tiled floors are still found in fine condition. Since the tiles are classically produced by hand—*fabrication artisanale*, in French—no two tiles are exactly alike in color or texture. This diversity creates a floor of subtly mottled beauty.

The terra-cotta floor suits the Norman climate perfectly. In this province, where shoes and boots often come in from outdoors wet, the moisture would soon ruin a rug, or a floor of wood parquet.

The long French windows of a room in the Château d'Audrieu near Bayeux are opened wide to let in a soft morning breeze, left. A variety of tiles are used to cover the floors of classic Norman houses, including 17th-century hand-hewn tiles of black *silex,* or flint, above right, and old hexagonal terracotta tiles, sometimes inset with white stone squares, above center and below.

Tiles can be quickly mopped up without suffering harm, even from a deluge. Parquet floors are occasionally used in Norman homes, but never on the ground floor. They appear in more luxurious dwellings in some bedrooms and hall landings. Stone floors—of flagstones, large granite tiles, or hewn "paving stones" of flint or limestone—cover many floors in the western part of Normandy.

An important central **stairway** is another feature typical of the classic two-story Norman house. Aside from the generously proportioned common room or living room, most rooms are somewhat small, designed for intimacy and warmth. Fireplaces are integral parts of the living room and the dining room, and usually of the kitchen and bedrooms as well, providing protective warmth against the cool damp climate.

The stairway leading to the upper floors of the Norman *manoir* is frequently paired with a sumptuous balustrade and banister of carved oak. Stairs are usually bordered and backed with oak or elm, and are filled in the center with terra-cotta tiling, though they may also be constructed entirely of richly patined oak. The extensive use of oak and terra-cotta throughout the interior of Norman dwellings creates an atmosphere of refined rusticity and warmth that exudes welcome.

The banister that encloses the central staircase in the 16th-century Château d'Harcourt in Le Neubourg is of graceful wrought iron on the lower floors, left, and cedes to majestically carved oak on the upper floors, right.

An elegant 18th-century fireplace enhances the dining room of the Châteaud'Audrieu, right, as does the delicate crystal chandelier.

The days of pedestals and prominence are long past for this odd lot of sculpted busts, above, discovered behind a closet door in the Château d'Harcourt.

The fine, reserved lines of a 17th-century fireplace in the Château d'Harcourt, right, reflect the strong and harmonious approach to design that appealed to architects in the 1600s.

Set against a mullioned window to catch the light, this 19th-century portrait, above, shows a Normandy matron in traditional dress.

In old Normandy the kitchen was always the warmest room in the house. Even in the modern home, the tones of copper and brick, and ancient wooden beams create an inviting environment. At right, a richly sculpted door separates the stone-tiled dining room from the heavy-beamed and antique-filled kitchen of this home in Upper Normandy. Old keys to various doors on the property and a pair of scissors hang on pegs at the kitchen door, below.

Antique copper pots and molds adorn the walls of this rustic but carefully equipped kitchen, right and below right, illuminated by a gleaming 18th-century bronze chandelier. Displayed above the kitchen door, below right, is a fine 18th-century Rouen faience platter. The large, late 17th-century cachepot to the left of the door is from Nevers.

As in the rest of the world, the bathrooms in Normandy have been updated and modernized for convenience. Yet sometimes, as in the bathroom at left and above, the original charm still exists. The room has its share of antiques, with an 18th-century pine commode displaying 19th-century pharmacy bottles, while a 17th-century oak chair holds a towel. A lone pink camellia, above, graces the sill of the bathroom's small window.

FURNITURE

The furniture of every province reflects the fortunes of its region. In times of austerity, the designs grow simpler, smaller, and less lavish, geared to function rather than form or appearance. In times of plenty, the furniture blossoms, and the pieces become more richly ornamented, larger, more finely crafted, more stylish.

In Normandy, furniture-making began to flourish in the 17th century with the rise in maritime commerce. By the 18th and 19th centuries the Normans were enjoying real prosperity, and it was apparent in the way they decorated their houses, whether they resided in a cottage, *manoir*, or château. Each piece of furniture was commissioned by and created for an individual or family, so that its size, shape, and adornment depended upon the client's resources and needs. The major centers for furniture production in the province were the agriculturally rich towns of Fécamp and Yvetot, as well as the area around Caen.

For the finest pieces, the wood of choice was always oak. Pine, softer and easier to sculpt, but knottier and more resinous, was reserved for humbler furniture. Occasionally elm, apple, chestnut, or beech was used. Mahogany, brought back from the Caribbean by Norman sailors, was highly prized, and was employed toward the end of the 18th century by cabinetmakers in towns near the ports of Upper Normandy, such as Rouen and Fécamp. There are even some examples of oak armoires that were stained to imitate the look of this treasured wood.

Undulating back support and a rush seat define this rare 18th-century side chair finely carved in oak, top. Above is a rare latticework *garde-manger*, or food storage cabinet, produced in pine in the early 1800s.

Built in the town of Lieuvin, the 18th-century oak *pétrin*, above, designed for the preparation of bread, has a hinged top to allow storage of rising dough within. The elegantly carved early 19th-century *buffet bas*, or low buffet, left, was produced in the Pays de Caux in Upper Normandy.

The simple lines of this rustic early 19th-century armchair, left, reflect its humble origins in a farming community. The 19th-century *armoirette de laiterie,* or small dairy armoire, below, was created in the Avranches region; the pierced sheet-iron door allows for aeration.

93

Norman furniture is distinguished by its elaborate carving. Two of the strongest decorative themes in the 18th and 19th centuries were prosperity and love. Cornucopias, bunches of grapes, sheaves of wheat, and baskets of flowers conveyed the plenty of the land. *L'amour* was frequently represented by such traditional symbols as hearts, a quiver and arrows, or two doves billing, while marriage was symbolized by a torch, and the family by a nest of birds. Other Norman motifs and designs include acanthus leaves, geometric patterns, farm implements, musical instruments, a pelican to show religious devotion, and anchors symbolizing the maritime vocations of the region's many navigators, fishermen, and sailors.

The cabinetmaker's skill as a sculptor soared when it came to embellishing a fine **armoire** for a wealthy client. Nothing is more representative of Norman furniture than an elaborately carved oak armoire. Before the accession of Louis XIV to the throne, in 1643, these pieces were small and modestly carved. But with the arrival of the luxe-loving "Sun King" and his vast stylistic influence, the Norman armoire developed into the imposing and richly carved masterwork that it has remained.

The cornices—either flat or, by the late 18th century, swelling sensuously upward in a *chapeau de gendarme*, or "policeman's hat," style—are embellished by several rows of decorative carving. Appliquéd under the cornices of some armoires made during and after the Louis XV period is an impressively carved and cutout ornament—a basket of flowers, a garland encircling two doves, an intricately detailed ensemble of wheat and grapes. The double rectangular doors are usually elegantly carved with flowers and vines in the corners, along the top, and, most ornately, on a wide band across

A majestic 18th-century desk, left, produced most likely near Fécamp, is carved with artistry and restraint. Like many antique Norman desks, it began life as a three-drawer farm table and was converted, by removing the center drawer, around 1900.

the middle. *Ferrures*, the decorative metalwork on the doors of many Norman cabinets, were exclusively of wrought iron until the mid-1800s, when copper hardware began to appear. Down the center of the 18th- and 19th-century armoires runs a sculpted pilaster. At the bottom of a very few armoires is a drawer, or sometimes two drawers, that runs the breadth of the piece.

Until the 18th century, armoires were almost entirely in the domain of the upper classes, but later they became common in the homes of peasants. Here in Normandy, as in other provinces, the armoire was the traditional wedding gift that the bride brought to her marriage, and thus was often carved with romantic motifs.

An étagère designed for storing tableware, the Norman *vaisselier* is built of oak, elm, and sometimes of cherry or pine. It usually has a straight, lightly sculpted cornice and shelving laid out with small sculpted railings to hold the china. Some *vaisseliers* have handmade hooks or nails on which to hang the cider cups called *moques*, while others are designed with slots to store and display large spoons above the dishes.

The *vaisselier* usually sits on a low **buffet** from which it is stepped back in a hutchlike arrangement. The buffet traditionally has two square, lightly ornamented doors and small curved legs. In some buffets two or three drawers are set in above the doors to store flatware.

Generally a rather long, rectangular, and rustic affair, the Norman **table** is distinctive only in its ample proportions and thick top. Constructed of oak or elm, such tables are usually supported by four or six sturdy square legs. Under a few tabletops is a sliding shelf, which, when extended, can function as a sideboard. Sometimes called harvest tables, or simply farm tables, these pieces were often accompanied by long simple benches rather than chairs. Only at the head of the table was there a

Carved of fine hard pine, this 19th-century flat-top armoire, left, originates in the Pays de Caux in upper Normandy.

The elegantly sculpted pine armoire, left, created in the 19th century, is distinguished by a graceful *chapeau de gendarme*—or policeman's hat—cornice. The 19th-century oak armoire, below, was produced in Rouen.

This 19th-century *horloge Saint-Nicolas,* or Saint Nicholas grandfather clock, below, is typical of the tall, thin clocks created in oak in the town of Aliermont.

high-backed armchair, often wide enough for two, which was designed for the master of the house.

The **chairs** of Normandy were more strongly influenced in design by the styles of Louis XIII, XIV, XV, and XVI than any other piece of furniture, and are thus less typically provincial than other Norman pieces. Norman chairs, especially after the 18th century, took several different forms: austerely designed banquettelike chairs, all in wood, with storage under the seat; small side chairs; deep-seated armchairs *à la bonne femme;* and armchairs with upholstered seats and arms. Many of the classic high-backed side chairs, crafted in cherry or oak, have rush seats, with the straw sometimes left natural, sometimes partially colored, with green or red strips alternating with the natural. The most characteristic chairback is designed with three carved and undulating *traverses,* or rungs, but there are also chairs backed with carved urns, sheafs of wheat, shells, or even medallions of animals.

The earliest Norman *horloges,* or **grandfather clocks,** were created for the *salle commune,* or living room, in the first half of the 18th century. Two major styles of clocks that appeared around the time of Louis XV have remained classics: the clock in the straight-sided, "coffin-shaped" casing, its top slightly larger than its bottom; and the clock with a nipped-in-at-the-waist or hourglass casing, called *la demoiselle* (the young lady), which has a wide oval, glass-windowed center portion set in below the narrowest point to accommodate the movement of the pendulum. Then, of course, there are the famous Saint-Nicolas clocks from the town of Saint-Nicolas-d'Aliermont, which are very tall, with narrow rectangular bodies and large, elaborately sculpted heads.

Created from oak, wild cherry, or pine, Norman clocks typically have faces of white enamel with black arabic or Roman numerals. Clockfaces designed in pewter or yellow copper are early and now very rare. On more ornate clocks the face is surrounded by an elaborately worked frame of embossed copper. The movements themselves, although sometimes made locally in Rouen or Dieppe, were more often brought in from outside the region—from the Jura, an alpine province to the east, or even from Switzerland.

Created from beech, this small painted chest, above, is one of many made in 19th-century Rouen, and then sold widely throughout Upper Normandy to fishermen and farmers.

A *lit clos,* or enclosed bed, such as the one at the right, created from oak in the 18th century, was a traditional piece of furniture in the homes of well-to-do farmers.

A rustic late—19th-century child's chair, below, is simply but sturdily designed.

This late—18th-century *trumeau,* or chimney-breast, above left, ornately carved in oak, was designed to top a mantle and complements an elegant room's woodwork. Carved from oak, this 19th-century *buffet-vaisselier,* or buffet with recessed étagères, far left, was designed to store and display faience and porcelain. The 19th-century *égouttoir,* or draining table, left, topped by a *vaisselier,* was used for drying dishes or sometimes cheeses.

The sumptuously detailed oak armoire on these pages, is in the collection of the Musée de Vieux Honfleur. Detailed with hearts, doves, and flowers, it is typical of armoires presented as wedding gifts.

NORMANDY'S ARTFUL DOMESTIC CRAFTS

Imagination, skill, and great care went into Normandy's legacy of finely crafted domestic objects. The baskets, butter molds, crocks, and plates—essential elements in day-to-day Norman life—were rarely created simply to fulfill their functions. For the proud Norman craftsman, perfectionist to the core, even these simple pieces had to have aesthetic value. Thus baskets were finely woven into singular shapes, butter molds were intricately carved with agricultural motifs, and plates, colorfully decorated on a white ground, were often finished with scalloped, fluted, or beaded borders.

Ceramics have been produced in Normandy since the Middle Ages, and continued to be an important industry into the 19th century. Several areas endowed with the two essentials of ceramic production—clay from sedimentary river banks and plentiful forests to fire the kilns—developed wide reputations for quality faience, among them the city of Rouen, Melamare in the Seine-Maritime, Infréville in the Eure, and Martincamp and Forges-les-Eaux in the Pays de Bray. Baskets were made by local weavers throughout Normandy, but the town of Remilly-sur-Lozon, where a three-hundred-year-old tradition of basketwork continues today, is a particularly well-known center.

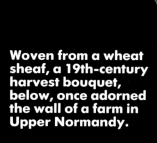

Woven from a wheat sheaf, a 19th-century harvest bouquet, below, once adorned the wall of a farm in Upper Normandy.

Round woven metal baskets, such as the one above, produced in the 19th century for drying salad or collecting eggs, could once be found in the kitchen of almost every Norman home.

A large farm basket, above, was used for harvesting in the 19th century.

A collection of 19th-century butter molds, below, from the Musée de Martainville, are carved in walnut with cows, turnips, cabbages, and strawberries, among other motifs.

A large 19th-century ceramic pot with dark brown glaze, left, part of a collection at the Musée de Martainville, is typical of pottery produced in the town of Martincamp. The finely woven Normand market basket, above, with two covers and a subtle diamond pattern in the weave, was created in the 19th century.

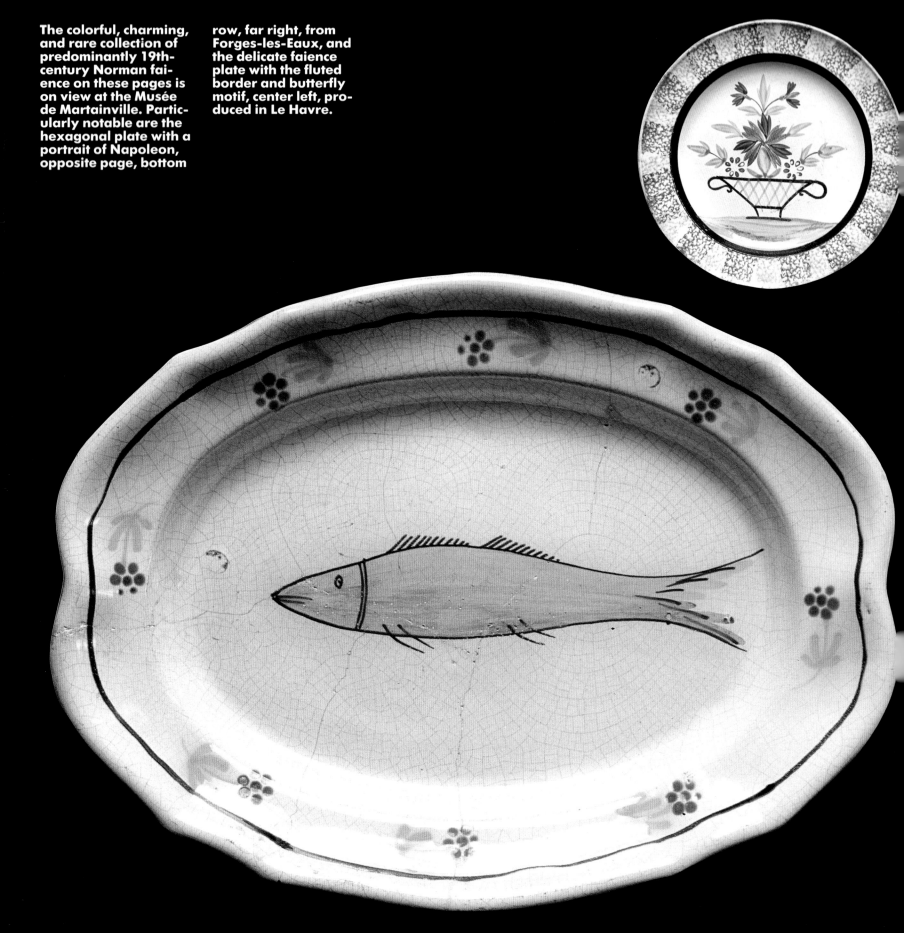

The colorful, charming, and rare collection of predominantly 19th-century Norman faience on these pages is on view at the Musée de Martainville. Particularly notable are the hexagonal plate with a portrait of Napoleon, opposite page, bottom row, far right, from Forges-les-Eaux, and the delicate faience plate with the fluted border and butterfly motif, center left, produced in Le Havre.

ARTISANAT
HANDCRAFTED THE NORMAN WAY

The Norman's taste for precision and perfection, and his tremendous pride in craftsmanship, are apparent in the decorative elements, the crafts, and the prosaic *objets* of Normandy's daily life, just as they are apparent in the region's architecture and furniture. With a few exceptions, notably the *faîtages*, or roof ornaments, and the lace, function rules form, but always with an eye for line and harmony. From a tiny, gleaming copper sauce pot to a colossal church bell, from a precious patch of lace to a mundane milk can, the artisanal production of Normandy is among the finest in France.

LACE

The wondrously complex laces of Normandy fall into two categories: *dentelle aux fuseaux*, or bobbin lace, and *point d'Alençon*, or needlepoint lace. Bobbin lace is the specialty of Bayeux, while Alençon, of course, is headquarters for the needlepoint lace that bears its name. Alençon lace is characterized by delicate appliqué—intricate designs stitched on a gossamer linen base as fragile as a spider's web. So fragile is it that the lace is traditionally "ironed" with the tip of a lobster claw. A piece of *point d'Alençon* smaller than a penny takes about sixteen hours to create. A five-inch circle of the lace takes one *dentellière* almost three months of full-time labor. For this reason, and because there are only about a dozen full-time lacemakers working in Alençon, the needlepoint lace of Normandy is almost priceless.

This exquisite handkerchief, left, created by Madame Salvador, the director of the Atelier du Centre Normand de la Dentelle aux Fuseaux, required 1,200 hours of work. Each *carte*, or design card, in this assortment, right, is perforated with a different pattern; the red cards are for creating white lace, the white cards for black lace.

In Bayeux, during the craft's 19th-century heyday, there were once about 5,000 lacemakers; today there are only ten, with about three score apprentices learning the craft. Bobbin lace is created by weaving and twisting from 50 to more than 600 threaded wooden bobbins around a blindingly intricate cluster of pins outlining the pattern on a velvet board. Bayeux lace, which can be black, white, or ecru, is figurative and floral, and is based on designs created in the 18th century. Traditionally, the lacemaking process here followed four steps: First, the artist conceived and drew the design on paper; then a *metteur en carte* transferred the design onto a card with tiny pinpricks, creating something like a perforated stencil; next a *maitresse dentellière*, or master lacemaker, parceled out the various pieces of a pattern to the army of lacemakers employed by the atelier (lacemaking expert and teacher Marie-Hélène Salvador relates that some women spent their entire working lives re-creating just one or two designs); in the final step, a *raboutisseuse,* or "joiner," stitched the finished parts of the pattern together to make an apparently seamless whole.

A small showroom in Bayeux's Atelier du Centre Normand de la Dentelle aux Fuseaux, where Madame Salvador, the Directrice, and others are committed to preserving the dying art of Bayeux lacemaking, displays beautiful examples of bobbin lace, such as handkerchiefs, borders, and collars. Some small pieces are for sale at prices that range from about sixty dollars to several hundred.

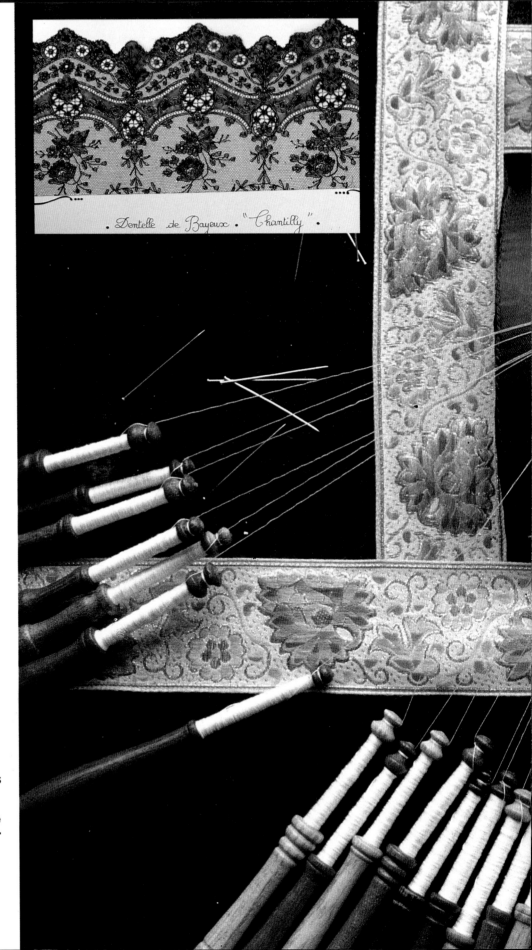

A fragile piece of black Bayeux lace, inset right, created in 1870, is part of the historical collection of the Centre Normand de la Dentelle aux Fuseaux. Lacemaking in progress: a web of threads attached to wooden bobbins spreads out around a bit of lace taking shape in Bayeux, right.

. Dentelle de Bayeux . "Chantilly" .

COIFS

Imaginative confections of lace, batiste, tulle, and wire, the coifs of Normandy represented a wide range of mood and spirit, as well as distinct local styles. In the Avranches region the *coiffe* was designed with two "wings," and was nicknamed "the butterfly." The "comet," from around Coutances, was a tall helmet of lace. A long, conical coif decorated with embroidered velvet was the headdress from the Caux region. Most of the excessively stylized coifs displayed today in museums date from the end of the 19th century—the showy *belle époque* period. The coifs were reserved for Sundays and holidays. For everyday wear the women of Normandy covered their heads with no-nonsense cotton bonnets of head-hugging sobriety.

In the windy environs of the Norman coast, how did these fragile, intricate, and sometimes lofty coifs remain anchored to the head? They were designed above, and sewn into, a tightly fitted linen toile cap, and were sometimes even stuck onto the forehead with paste and tied around a chignon in the back. Then a long decorative pin, like an oversized hatpin, was set into the coif from the top and fixed in the cap or the hair, stabilizing the headdress as well as adorning it with an enamel flower or little metal balls.

The voluminous late-19th-century coif is from the Pays d'Auge, left. A lady in Lower Normandy wears a regional coif, above. The intricately embroidered linen bonnets, right, are from the Musée du Vieux Honfleur and are typical of head coverings once designed for everyday wear.

FAÎTAGES

The *épis de faîtage*—literally, roof-ridge spikes—are the unusual tall ceramic ornaments that crown the peaks of many Norman roofs and dormer windows. They are distinctly and characteristically regional. Many designs were and still are created in dazzling enameled colors and sinuous shapes: cats, roosters, doves, griffins and other fantasy birds, elongated vases, sculpted female heads, fruits, and geometric forms. Some *faîtages* are like totem poles in their towering vertical piling-on of shapes, colors, and motifs. The care and artistry that go into the *épis de faîtage* can never be fully appreciated once they are installed—sixty or a hundred feet above the ground, they are simply too far away for the viewer to grasp their gorgeous detail. Small roof-ridge tiles called *tuiles faitières*—*faitière* in French pertains to the roof's ridge or peak—run the entire length of the peak, and were designed in the form of fleurs-de-lis, balls, or spear tips, giving the rooftop a bristly look from afar.

A romantic fad that developed in the mid-19th century in Calvados, the *faîtages* were most likely

Elaborate ceramic ornaments, called *faî-tages,* adorn almost every roof corner of the Hotel Normandy in Deauville. Each a finely finished example of the ceramist's craft, *faî-tages* such as the stork, left, and the squirrel, below, are almost impossible to appreciate from ground level.

A ceramic cat stalks the rooftops of Deauville, opposite page left. Maurice Barbé, who helps out his son, J. J. Barbé, in his porcelain and pottery business in Touques, displays one of the company's glazed *faîtages,* opposite page right.

113

inspired by the ceramics that decorated Renaissance dwellings. They were produced on a grand scale after 1870 to top the roofs of stylish villas and *manoirs.* These colorful *objets* serve absolutely no functional purpose—they are purely, blatantly decorative. No one at the turn of the century, a time of preoccupation with appearances and display among the upper classes, would consider his villa in Cabourg or Deauville complete without the opulent adornment of the *épis* at every peak and corner of his roof. After 1914, the *faîtage* trend quickly waned, though roof ornaments are still made today in the Calvados region, in towns near the coast.

The tall *épis* are made up of various components assembled atop an iron shank that is fixed to the rooftop. The base piece is cemented to the roof, while the others are stacked on top and fixed with tar or oily rags, making the assembled *épis* supple enough to withstand the seasonal winds.

The sea along the Côte Fleurie, which extends from Trouville to Cabourg, stretches out below a large ceramic rooster, left. A pensive monkey crouched at a roof peak, above, displays the rich polychrome glazes that characterize the best *faîtages.*

THE BELLS OF NORMANDY

The Cornille-Havard bell foundry—Le Fonderie de Cloches—has been making pitch-perfect cast bells for more than 200 years, but the tradition of bell-making in Villedieu-les-Poêles is seven hundred years older than that. The Knights of Saint John, skilled in metalwork, returned from Jerusalem in the 12th century and settled in Siennetre, a town just a few miles from Mont-Saint-Michel. These religious *chevaliers*, under the protection of the Knights of Malta, renamed the town Villedieu (God's town); "les poêles" (the pans) was added on to the name several years later. The Knights established an industry that is still flourishing, using techniques that have changed little over the ensuing centuries.

Each bell, cast in bronze, is created to sound several notes at the same time—the fundamental note, the hum note an octave below, the nominal

The cast bronze sign at the door of the Cornille Havard bell foundry invites visitors to ring and enter, above.

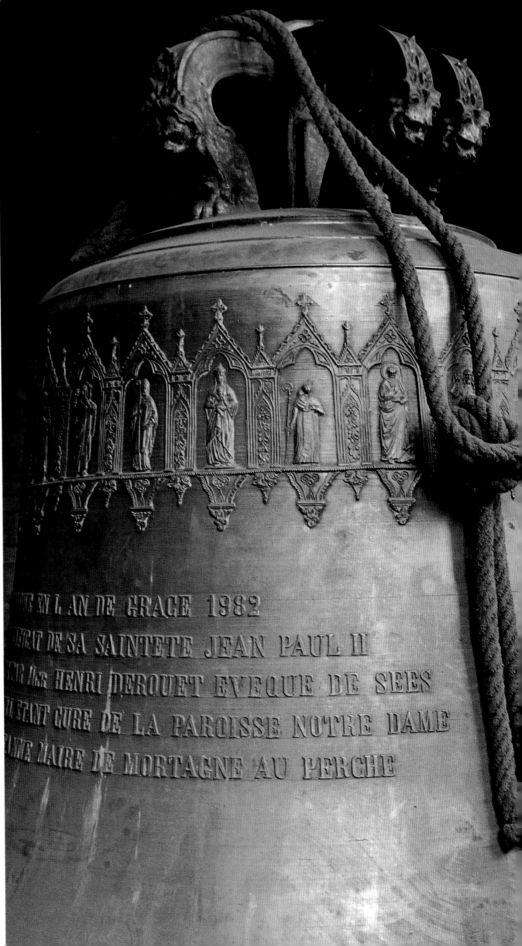

A huge customized bell, right, awaits a final polishing in the atelier of the Fonderie de Cloches in Villedieu-les-Poêles.

A group of bells in various stages of completion, right, have been created to comply with a client's specifications for size and melody.

an octave above, a minor third, and a fifth. The average bell weighs more than 600 pounds, and generally is as tall as it is wide. The tone of the bell depends on the diameter of the bell at the bottom and the ratio of the thickness of the metal to the diameter. A handful of foundry men do the molding, casting, and polishing, a slow, meticulous, and ancient process. One false move results in one false note, or, perhaps, no note at all.

The bells of the Cornille-Havard foundry are cast, singly or in melodic groups of up to ten or more, for institutions and individuals around the world. Bells can be ordered by size, by note, or, in a group, by melody. According to the client's wishes, every bell is decorated and personalized in the casting with floral garlands, geometric patterns, biblical phrases, inscriptions, or proper names. The foundry is open for visits, and an hour passed here is an hour spent back in a time when the world moved more slowly and when quality was more important than quantity.

The used and damaged clay molds, above, resemble a massive modern sculpture.

In the Fonderie's main hall, right, visitors get an idea of the bell-making process from descriptive wall diagrams and later from observing various stages of production.

A handful of foundry workers, such as the employee, right, produce the celebrated bells of Villedieu-les-Poêles using techniques that have changed little since the Middle Ages.

COPPERWARE

Sharing a history and early traditions with the Fonderie de Cloches, the copperware industry in Villedieu-les-Poêles also has its roots in the Middle Ages, when the metalworking Knights of Saint John arrived there. Pots and pans, urns and pitchers, pails, milk cans, and utensils of copper have been continuously produced for nine hundred years in this quaint little town, where masses of copper shine from almost every storefront.

Two major copper ateliers dominate the town today, Lucien Lecellier's and Étienne Dulin's. The Lecellier enterprise, a seventh-generation business on the outskirts of town, is a mechanized and well-orchestrated operation in which much of the work is done by machine. Monsieur Dulin's establishment, founded in 1920, is set off the main street right in the center of Villedieu. It's installed in one of the town's oldest copperware workrooms, with rough-hewn gray stone walls, cobbled floors, and exposed beams. Here, in the Atelier du Cuivre, which is open by arrangement to visitors, all the work is still done by hand, in keeping with old techniques and traditions.

In Étienne Dulin's Atelier du Cuivre, all the copperware, such as this generously proportioned pot, left, is made entirely by hand. Copper and tin filings stored in a back shed form a shimmering metallic still life *chez* Dulin, inset left.

IMPLEMENTS AND ELEMENTS OF COUNTRY LIFE

Even the most functional and mundane of agricultural objects—a milk can, for example—has definite appeal when it is created with the understanding of harmony, line, and proportion that marks all Norman handicrafts. A gracefully designed picket fence in a village near Honfleur encloses a soft green pasture and adds to its allure, while a delicate wrought-iron fence in Victot-Pontfol enhances an orchard. Farm implements and the accoutrements of rural life in Normandy are a happy marriage between exacting functional needs and individual fantasy—a union that nevertheless remains grounded in ancestral tradition.

In the Suisse Normande and other rural parts of Normandy, empty milk cans are set out at the gate in the evening, left, ready to be picked up and replaced by full ones early the next morning. On the property of the Hostellerie du Moulin du Pré, a small inn in Bavent, flowers peep over the top of a sturdy weathered barrel, right. Overleaf: A drive along rural Norman lanes reveals a variety of rustic and charming farm gates; both wood pickets and wrought-iron bars enclose properties that stretch on for acres.

COUNTRY FARE

The sensuously thick, satiny smooth *crème fraîche* of the Norman countryside and the sweet juicy apples whose trees define the landscape are the two great inspirations of Norman gastronomy. The bane of a dieter's existence, the cuisine of Normandy is one of the richest in France. Fish, shellfish, meat, and game are flavored, flamed, or garnished with butter, cream, milk, cider, Calvados, and apples in dizzying and divine variations. The cheeses that follow the main course and precede dessert—the celebrated Camembert, the Pont-l'Évêque, the Pavé d'Auge, and the Livarot—are almost a meal in themselves, served with fresh crusty bread and sometimes fruit. The ingredients are always of the highest quality, originating as they do in the province's fields, farms, and offshore waters. Delicately flavored mussels; the plump, briny oysters of Saint-Vaast-la-Hougue; lobsters just off the boat; grass-fed young lambs; farm-raised ducks and rabbits; the tenderest veal—the local products are incomparable. Normandy is a gourmand's dream fulfilled.

Classic regional dishes include *côte de veau au Calvados et à la crème*—veal chop in a Calvados-and-cream sauce; *poulet Vallée d'Auge*—sautéed chicken with apples in a Calvados-and-cream sauce; *soles normandes*—a fillet of sole bathed in butter, *crème fraîche*, cider, white wine and Calvados; *lapin au cidre*—rabbit marinated for several hours before braising in cider, vinegar, and Calvados; and two irresistible apple desserts, *crêpes flambées aux pommes*—thin pancakes with apples served in a flaming liquor sauce—and *tarte chaude normande*, beautiful concentric circles of apples baked in a golden crust and served with a pot of *crème fraîche*.

The finest Norman cooking remains straightforward and provincial in the best sense—copious, rich, succulent, and uncontrived. *Nouvelle cuisine* would be anathema to the spirit of Normandy.

Freshly cut garden flowers stand in a white country vase above a plate of pears in a country kitchen in Touques, left.

The striking bar of Les Deux Tonneaux, a small bistro lodged in a 17th-century cottage in the hamlet of Pierrefitte-en-Auge, left, is decorated with two massive Calvados casks, vertical beams, and a collection of cider pitchers. Here a wedge of local cheese accompanies the glass of cider.

An antique grandfather clock, a display of gleaming yellow-copper pots over the fireplace, and red-checked tablecloths accent the rustic, wood-beamed interior of Les Deux Tonneaux, right.

LES DEUX TONNEAUX

Under the flowering apple trees in the backyard, or on long farm tables next to the fireplace inside, Les Deux Tonneaux offers the simplest of Norman fare —crepes, fried eggs and ham, tripe, roasted free-range chicken, and apple tarts—in an atmosphere of rustic perfection. Monsieur Morel serves the food to his customers while Madame Morel prepares it in the back. The eggs come from the chickens next door; the apples have been plucked from the trees down the lane. Set in the center of Pierrefitte-en-Auge, a hamlet of thatched cottages, undulating fields, and apple orchards, Les Deux Tonneaux is the embodiment of the perfect rural spot every traveler to France hopes to discover. While you wait for a table you can have a drink at the bar, a massive, rough-hewn, 300-year-old tree trunk. Every window offers a view of orchards and cow pastures. On the hour, the bells from the little stone church across the road ring out.

A simple sign among the flowers outside the door, far left, signals the entrance to the classic Norman cottage, above, where a light lunch might consist of three vibrantly fresh farm eggs, crusty bread, a slice of Camembert, and a tumbler of cider, left.

BRASSERIE LES VAPEURS

It is eight on Friday night and you've just pulled into Deauville for the weekend. Is there a question about where you will have supper? There is not, since of course you will go to Les Vapeurs in Trouville, the bright and busy bistro in the town across the bridge, a pleasant resort in its own right but the other side of the tracks as far as Deauville is concerned.

The Brasserie Les Vapeurs is a local institution, currently owned and run by Martine and Gérard Bazire, an energetic and exacting couple whose home is featured on pages 208–221. The house specialties *aux Vapeurs* are the *moules*, either *marinière*—simmered with onions, vinegar, and butter —or *à la crème* (with cream), and the *crevettes à la vapeur*, the steamed shrimp. For dessert, many regulars look no farther than the *tarte tatin*, the warm, luscious, upside-down apple tart.

Martine and Gérard Bazire, proprietors of Les Vapeurs, take a momentary break, above, in front of their popular brasserie in Trouville. A pot of voluptuously rich *crème fraîche* accompanies both the *tarte tatin,* a warm upside-down apple tart, and a dish of fresh strawberries, right, two desserts of choice at Les Vapeurs.

The look and ambience at Les Vapeurs—stylish, convivial, loud—could not have been more felicitously conceived by Claude Lelouch. Everything about it is pure bistro—the saffron-colored walls; the old posters; the whimsical, dated neon signs; the long bar, in polished wood, and decked with a huge spray of bright flowers; the waiters and waitresses in traditional black uniforms with white aprons; the narrow tables packed together along the walls. Here you dine elbow to elbow with your neighbors, and it is not unusual to find yourself in their conversation, or them in yours. The crowd in season is well dressed, sometimes boisterous, invariably fun to watch.

Les Vapeurs is unpretentious but not entirely unself-conscious. It is simple, but it is "in." The limited menu of consistently good seafood (steaks and chops, too) and the warm and cheerful aura bring back the customers week after week, season after season. You feel happy here, you feel comfortable (though occasionally jostled), and after three visits you feel like a habitué.

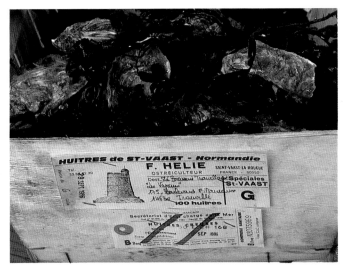

Cases of fresh oysters from St. Vaast-La Hougue, above, are delivered several times a week to the brasserie. The most popular dish at Les Vapeurs is the savory bowl of steaming _moules marinières,_ mussels in broth, right, sometimes served _à la crème,_ or with cream.

A worker from the neighboring fish market drops by Les Vapeurs for a brief lunchtime libation, left.

Les Vapeurs, left, established in 1927, is bustling throughout the year, especially on weekends, when every table is full.

LE PAVÉ D'AUGE

The town of Beuvron-en-Auge consists of little more than two intersecting roads lined with small, antique, half-timbered houses. In the spring and summer, wisteria vines frame doorways and windows. In the fall, the facades are abloom with geraniums. The center of this little hamlet, a 16th-century restored village, is dominated by the old covered market, today the site of the fine and warmly atmospheric restaurant Le Pavé d'Auge.

Odile Engel, a native of Alsace, discovered Beuvron-en-Auge, and the region of Calvados, on a family vacation in Normandy several years ago. Shortly thereafter, she and her husband bought the old marketplace, renovated it, and opened Le Pavé d'Auge, named both for a popular local cheese and for the town's antique cobblestones. The massively beamed interior beckons with a huge stone fireplace, a tiled floor, paneled walls, pink tablecloths, and little bouquets of flowers everywhere.

"I fell in love with Beuvron-en-Auge as soon as I saw it," relates Odile. "With its flowers and half-timbered houses, it had a touch of Alsace to it. But I was ready, nevertheless, for a change from Alsace. I had been working as a chef for twelve years there, preparing mainly Alsatian specialties. How long can one go on cooking *choucroute,* quiche, and *coq au Riesling?* Here in Beuvron I could cook what I wanted with some of the best fresh ingredients in the world!"

An intense and vigorous woman who is passionate about her métier, Odile Engel does all the marketing and cooking herself, while her husband acts as manager and host and her daughter as a waitress and assistant manager. The kitchen of Le Pavé d'Auge is modest and not spectacularly equipped. Odile works with some pieces of professional restaurant equipment, but more often she relies on the kind of tools, little jars, and pots that might be found in any woman's kitchen. Yet from out of this simple kitchen comes a menu that offers tantalizing choices. Should one take oysters in cider? A lobster flan? The succulent local fish, Saint Pierre, in a fresh tomato and butter sauce? A salmon fillet with oysters? *Poulet Vallée d'Auge* (chicken with apples, cream, and Calvados)? Or how about the breast of duck with foie gras?

"I don't make '*grande cuisine,*'" Odile Engel states, "but rather a '*cuisine du marché,*' with a menu that varies with the best that the day's market has to offer. We buy beautiful products and prepare them honestly, with a good quality/price rapport—and we are full all the time!"

Odile Engel, left, turns out tantalizing regional specialties in her small and simple kitchen. At the Pavé d'Auge, in the restored village of Beuvron-en-Auge, Odile Engel's refined *cuisine du marché,* or market-inspired menu, includes a delectable *Saint Pierre au Beurre de Tomates,* right.

SAINT PIERRE AU BEURRE DE TOMATES

John Dory in Tomato-Butter Sauce

- **4 medium-sized ripe tomatoes, about 2 pounds**
- **6 ounces sweet butter, about 1½ sticks**
- **Salt and pepper**
- **4 fillets of John Dory, skinned, or similar fleshy fish, such as red snapper, about ½ pound each**

1. Bring several quarts of water to a boil. Add the tomatoes. Boil for 3 minutes. Plunge tomatoes into cold water. Drain. Peel, quarter, and remove inside pulp and seeds. (Reserve for a tomato sauce.) Chop outside meat of the tomatoes.

2. Put the tomatoes in a 9-inch skillet and set over medium-high heat. Whisk in 2 tablespoons of butter, cook until tomatoes are very soft and evaporate their liquid. Then start whisking in 6 tablespoons of butter, 1 tablespoon at a time. Season with salt and pepper.

3. Melt the remaining butter in a nonstick skillet and sauté fish over medium heat, about 4 minutes on each side.

4. Nap the center of each plate with half the sauce and set the fillets on top; pour remaining sauce over fish. Serve with a bright vegetable, such as a carrot-and-bell-pepper puree, and garnish with fresh basil, chervil, or chives.

Makes 4 servings

Note: John Dory is better known in Europe as Saint Peter's fish. American John Dory is found from Nova Scotia to Cape Hatteras.

POULET VALLÉE D'AUGE

Chicken in Calvados
Cream Sauce

- 6 tablespoons (¾ stick) sweet butter
- 1 teaspoon salt
- 1 chicken, about 4 pounds, cut into quarters
- ½ cup Calvados
- 2 cups *crème fraîche,* or heavy cream
- 4 apples, Jonathan or Golden Delicious, cored, peeled, and thickly sliced
  Freshly ground pepper

1. Preheat oven to 400°F.
2. Smear 3 tablespoons butter over chicken pieces and season with ½ teaspoon salt.
3. Place chicken in roasting pan just large enough to fit chicken comfortably. Roast in middle oven 1 to 1¼ hours. Baste occasionally.
4. Set chicken on a preheated serving platter and keep warm. Drain excess fat.
5. Set pan over high heat, add ¼ cup Calvados, and reduce heat to medium. As soon as Calvados starts bubbling, ignite with a match, shaking pan until flames subside. Deglaze pan with crème fraîche, scraping caramelized drippings. Reduce sauce to 1¼ cups.
6. Meanwhile, melt remaining 3 tablespoons butter in a skillet over high heat, and sauté the apple slices until golden, about 3 minutes. Add remaining ¼ cup of Calvados. Cover and cook over medium for 5 minutes. Sprinkle with pepper.
7. Arrange chicken pieces on individual plates, spoon the sauce over them, arrange apples, and serve.

Makes 4 servings

Poulet Vallée d'Auge, **above left, and Madame Engel's** *huitres au cidre,* **left, use traditional ingredients.**

HUITRES AU CIDRE
Oysters in Cider Sauce

32 **medium-sized oysters on the half shell**
½ **cup imported French dry cider, approximately**
½ **cup *crème fraîche* or heavy cream, approximately**
4 **cups kosher salt**

1. Have oysters shucked at fish market. Reserve shells and liquor.

2. Measure amount of liquor; measure same amount of cream and same amount of cider.

3. Rinse oyster shells under cold water, then dry. Place an oyster in each shell.

4. Mix oyster liquor with cider and cream for the sauce. In a saucepan, cook mixture over medium heat until reduced to about ⅔ cup. Let it cool.

5. In a large broiler pan, pour kosher salt and make nest for each shell to keep them from tipping. Cover each oyster with sauce.

6. Preheat oven to 500°. Bake oysters for 5 to 6 minutes, until the tops are glazed brown.

7. Arrange the oysters on individual plates covered with kosher salt and serve immediately.

Makes 4 servings

Note: No seasoning is needed, says Odile Engel; the salt in the seawater is sufficient.

A soft pink tablecloth is the background for the Pavé d'Auge's enticing appetizer of marinated salmon, right.

A CHEESE CRAFTSMAN

Henri Pennec bills himself as a *maître artisan fromager,* a master cheese craftsman, and winner of numerous gold medals. Yet he is too modest. He is also a poet, and his verses embellish the wrappings of all his cheeses.

Monsieur Pennec, along with his wife, Janine, can be found every Saturday morning in Honfleur behind a stand at the weekly open market in the main square of this old port town. Sprouting from between and behind the cheeses is a garden of risqué couplets, inspired by cheese and love, displayed on hand-lettered cardboard squares. "Voluptuous Aphrodite," "The Butcher of Rouen," "The Stinky Norman," and "A Kick in the Pants" are just a few of the titles in Monsieur Pennec's repertoire.

At his Ranch Saint Sylvestre, Henri Pennec claims to create more than thirty kinds of cheeses—young ones, old ones, flavored ones, plain ones. The cheeses of this region are concentrated and intense: to make one square Pavé d'Auge cheese, Monsieur Pennec explains, requires six and a half liters of milk. The cheeses are aged for many months, and the best of them are unpasteurized (which means that they cannot be exported to the United States because of strict Food and Drug Administration laws).

The storerooms and workrooms of Monsieur Pennec's *fromagerie* are almost overpoweringly odoriferous—not surprisingly, given the number of cheeses within, in varying stages of ripeness or rankness. Asked if he was not occasionally bothered by the smell of cheese, Monsieur Pennec replied, "No, actually for me something smells bad when it *doesn't* smell of cheese!"

An assortment of local cheeses from the Pays d'Auge, left, ripen in the aging room of Henri Pennec's Ranch Saint Sylvestre near Honfleur. Monsieur Pennec, inset left, inspects all the cheeses daily, and frequently brushes the riper cheeses to remove mold from their skins.

LIVING IN NORMANDY

Nature is very close to the heart and soul of the traditional Norman home. In this fecund region of forests and fields, dwellings from the Pays de Caux to the Cotentin are carefully landscaped to augment the natural beauty of the surroundings with rustic rock gardens, lush *potagers* (vegetable gardens), rose-lined paths, and garlanded vines of wisteria. Inside the house, vases of fresh flowers are paired with the rich earth tones of patined wood and burnished terracotta—exterior elements that create a glowingly warm and inviting interior environment. If the house is on the coast, ideally the sea is always within sight, its tides and tempests visible directly beyond French doors leading onto a balcony. Within the residence, accents of blue and beige and perhaps some fish motifs recall the sea outside. ❦ Home to the hardworking Norman is a refuge from the cool wet climate and a

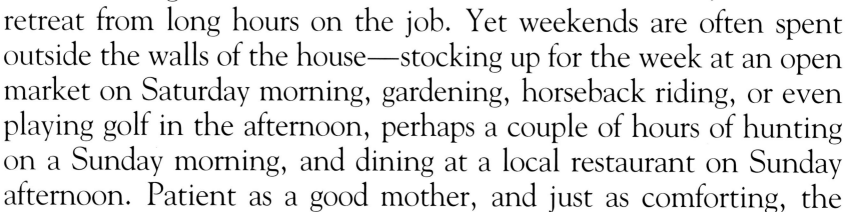

retreat from long hours on the job. Yet weekends are often spent outside the walls of the house—stocking up for the week at an open market on Saturday morning, gardening, horseback riding, or even playing golf in the afternoon, perhaps a couple of hours of hunting on a Sunday morning, and dining at a local restaurant on Sunday afternoon. Patient as a good mother, and just as comforting, the

house awaits the family's return. ❦ After a visit to the captivating Norman port town of Honfleur, with its splendid Saturday-morning market, "Living in Normandy" presents seven distinctly different homes, each unique in spirit and singular in decorative approach. From an impeccably restored 15th-century *manoir* near the thriving town of Lisieux to a contemporary apartment in the coastal resort town of Trouville, the homes reveal the taste and style of Normandy today.

At the end of the day, old wooden fishing barques line the quay in Honfleur beneath a zigzag skyline of pitched roofs, right.

HONFLEUR
A SMALL TOWN IN NORMANDY

The somber slate-sided facades and pitched roof-lines that distinguish the picturesque port town of Honfleur seem to change their hues with every turn in the weather. The profoundly deep gray grows more intense as leaden storm clouds roll in from the sea. It is as if the slate itself were absorbing pigment from the clouds. Under a dome of blue sky and an unimpeded sun, the slate softens and lightens in tone, turning dove gray or crystal gray, and sometimes looking like mica as it reflects the direct sun.

Honfleur's tall, narrow houses (some have seven stories!), its thriving and colorful fishing port, and its quaint, winding cobbled streets continue to inspire artists and writers, as they have for more than a century. Baudelaire wrote *Invitation au Voyage* in Honfleur, while he was living there with his ailing mother. He frequently walked to the port along the Rue de la Bavole, a street that Monet depicted in a canvas by that name in 1866. In that same year, Seurat was down at the docks painting his misty monochromatic port scene, *La Maria, Honfleur.* Boudin, Louis-Alexandre Dubourg, Johan Jongkind, Corot, Courbet, and later Braque all portrayed Honfleur in their very particular styles, colors, and moods. "Honfleur," wrote Baudelaire, "has always been the dearest of my dreams." Today the quays of the Vieux Basin (or Old Harbor), the cobbled *ruelles,* and the lively marketplace still

A slate-faced, slate-roofed house in Honfleur, right, is one of a score of landmark dwellings that line the harbor.

draw artists from throughout the world. At any given moment in the late spring or summer, a stroll around the port after lunch at L'Absinthe or L'Ancrage will reveal the town rendered in oils, pastels, gouache, charcoal, and pencil on a score of easels and sketch pads.

Honfleur is an ancient town whose recorded history goes back to the 11th century. It came to prominence in the early 17th century when the navigator and explorer Samuel de Champlain, a Dieppe shipbuilder, set sail for Canada from the port of Honfleur in 1608. A plaque near the port commemorates the departure and Champlain's subsequent founding of Quebec. Honfleur grew and prospered in the 17th and 18th centuries, becoming an important commercial and maritime port, and a center for foreign trade. Discovered and claimed by the impressionists in the 19th century, Honfleur remains a romantic town of great charm, little changed in a century.

Once occupied primarily by those in the maritime trades, the slate-faced and half-timbered houses that line the narrow streets are now home to lawyers, doctors, artists, merchants, teachers, and tourism executives as well as to those whose occupations continue to be tied to the sea. The most interesting streets for gazing upon the architecture of old Honfleur are the rue Haute, the former *quartier* of the town's rich shipbuilders, the rue de l'Homme de Bois, the rue de la Bavole, the rue du Puits, the rue Brulée, the streets along the port, and two pedestrian streets—the rue de la Prison and the rue de la Ville. Accenting the intriguing exteriors are pretty lace-curtained windows and whimsical hand-painted signs suspended above the entrances to museums, restaurants, boutiques, and even the local unemployment office.

A fishing boat from Honfleur's colorful fleet pulls out for a day at sea, right.

146

In the heart of town is the Place Sainte-Catherine, an open, cobbled square dominated by the striking and unusual landmark church, L'Église Sainte-Catherine. Constructed entirely of wood in the late 15th and early 16th centuries, the church is unique in that it was not built by architects and masons, but rather was designed and built by local chandlers, using the means and methods of their trade. The two vaulted interior naves are constructed like the upturned hulls of great twin ships, set in perpetual, celestial dry dock. Massive, roughly squared beams hewn from local trees support the naves. The interior walls are half-timbered in the style of the Pays d'Auge. As the result of an uncommon but eminently practical architectural decision, the belfry does not crown the church's roof, but instead stands alone, set facing the church across the square. It is likely that the bell tower was built separately because the chandlers feared that the church's wooden construction would not bear the weight of the bells. Timbered and shingled, the bell tower leans on eight crutch-like struts, giving the steeple an awkward appearance but at the same time the strength to withstand the vicissitudes of five centuries.

Also facing the church is an old wood-shingled inn and restaurant, the Hostellerie du Chat, where guests can tell the time by the bells of Sainte-Catherine. Winding off from the Place Sainte-Catherine are little streets such as the rue des Logettes and the rue des Lingots, where antiques shops, galleries, and boutiques offer the visitor a fascinating variety of merchandise, from antique

A street near the port, below, is banked by tall and somber slate buildings, one of which still advertises an archaic remedy for seasickness on the shingles above the pharmacy.

An assortment of spring flowers on sale in Place Sainte-Catherine, left, where a market of fresh produce is held every Saturday.

A large clock framed in sculpted stone, right, keeps time atop the *mairie*, or town hall, for the citizens of Honfleur.

sextants, model boats, old postcards, and Art Deco lamps to impressionistic contemporary oils of local landscapes and seascapes.

The Musée Eugène Boudin is set off the rue de L'Homme de Bois, a few minutes' walk up from the Place Sainte-Catherine. A modern but architecturally uninspired homage to Boudin and his fellow impressionists of the Saint Siméon school, the museum displays, in addition to the works of these 19th-century masters, some Norman costumes, furniture, and coifs. A museum with more character and color is the Musée du Vieux Honfleur—the Museum of Old Honfleur—which is really two museums across a cobbled alley from each other. One, the Musée de la Marine, lodged in a former church, offers a wonderful collection of model boats and other seafaring memorabilia, while the other, the Musée d'Ethnographie et d'Art Populaire—the Folk Art Museum—houses antique regional furniture, a large collection of handcrafted objects and utensils from Norman domestic life, 18th-century tiles from the Pays d'Auge, and 19th-century coifs, displayed in twelve intimate rooms.

The liveliest time of the week in Honfleur is Saturday morning, when the town's weekly open market covers the Place Sainte-Catherine with rows of stands and stalls and vendors hawking everything from fresh goat cheese to apple-blossom nosegays

This colorful hand-painted sign, left, on the rue de l'Homme de Bois marks the entrance to the local unemployment office. Another sign, below, represents a 19th-century sailing ship.

and plump live rabbits. The market overflows the *place* and spills into the side streets and down the wide steps that lead to the port. The vivid splashes of color from the piles of tomatoes, the mounds of green beans, and especially from the multihued bouquets plucked from the gardens of local farmers brighten, if only for a moment, the old streets and dark facades. Honfleur's Saturday market is the place to buy the makings of a bountiful picnic— four or five kinds of *charcuterie,* several salads, two kinds of bread, four cheeses, a basket of fruit, a freshly baked *tarte,* some lacy cookies, and a small box of chocolate truffles—to lay out later in a bosky glen or on the beach of Deauville.

Many artists set up their easels along the quays of Honfleur's old port, above left and right, to capture the colors, the light, and the architecture in a variety of media. Fledgling artists, left, sketch on the steps of the church of Sainte Catherine. Overleaf: The Saturday-morning market on the Place Sainte-Catherine, where one can buy anything from a nosegay of apple blossoms to plump live rabbits, is a kaleidoscope of bright, lively vignettes.

le Trouville "Deauville"

Vierges Folles
Tour
Retard
on Amour
Paris

MON COEUR TOUT EMBAUME
PAR L'IODE DES ALGUES
LES CARESSES D'EMBRUNS
ET LES HERBES CHOISIES
VIENT VOUS ENTRETENIR
D'UN MURMURE DE VAGUES
DES PLAGE AU SABLE FIN
DE LA COTE FLEURIE.

FROMAGE IODE

Among the glimpses of life seen through the windows of the quay-side buildings, young chefs labor in the second-floor kitchen of a harbor-view restaurant, right.

Pretty, tree-shaded country roads wander through the outskirts of Honfleur and lead to superb panoramic viewpoints and endearing little neighboring villages. Driving along the Côte de Grâce, which runs through the hills above the town, one comes to a beautiful 17th-century country chapel, Notre Dame de Grâce. It was to this graceful and elegant stone church that the great French navigators came to pray before setting off on voyages to explore the New World. There is a wonderful view across the Seine estuary to Le Havre from the nearby Calvary. Down the road, the Mont-Joli viewpoint offers a fine vista of the town below and the neighboring hills. Barneville-la-Bertran is a tiny hamlet four miles from Honfleur that is also worth a visit to see its old church with Romanesque tower and haunting *temps perdu* cemetery, and perhaps to have lunch in the garden of the Auberge de la Source.

The pastoral road banked by apple orchards that leads from Honfleur to Trouville is a lovely eight-mile drive that takes one through the minuscule hamlets of Vasouy, Pennedepie, Cricqueboeuf (with its 12th-century church and duck pond), and Villerville, with one of France's smallest self-contained *mairies,* or town halls—about the size of an apartment kitchen, and open for business two hours a week. Beyond Trouville, a turn-of-the-century resort, lies Deauville, the sophisticated playground of the horsey set, so different in spirit, ambience, and character from the venerable port of Honfleur.

The small streets of Honfleur, right top to bottom, once walked by visitors such as Baudelaire, Monet, and Corot, are lined with small, beguiling old houses and antiques shops.

155

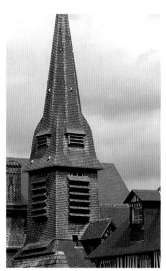

Within Honfleur's landmark wood church, Sainte-Catherine's, the naves, above, are constructed like the upturned hulls of a ship. The church's bell tower, left, built separately, faces the church from across the *place*. In the alcove dedicated to Saint Anthony, right, plaques of thanks attest to many prayers answered.

Notre Dame de Grâce, right, is an enchanting 17th-century country chapel set on a hillside above Honfleur overlooking the Seine estuary. It was here that the region's great navigators once came to pray before setting off to discover new worlds.

Cette Chapelle, construite en 1600 – 1615
par les bourgeois et marins de Honfleur
sur un terrain donné par Mme de Montpensier,
Remplace une ancienne Chapelle
fondée avant l'an 1023
par Richard II, duc de Normandie,
Et disparue dans un éboulement de la côte
au XVIe siècle.

Août 1902. — Société le Vieux-Honfleur

The plaque above explains: "This chapel was built between 1600 and 1615 by the merchants and seamen of Honfleur on land donated by Madame de Montpensier. It replaces an ancient chapel founded before the year 1023 by Richard II, duke of Normandy, and lost in a landslide in the 16th century." Stone-sculpted molding, friezes, and statues, above right, far right, and right, embellish the facade of this isolated little chapel.

Near the Musée du Vieux Honfleur, two small signs, left, point the way to the old salt storehouse and to the alley that once ran by the town prison. Samuel de Champlain set off for his 17th-century explorations of the New World, and subsequent founding of Quebec, not far from this quay in Honfleur's old port, right.

GRENIERS A SEL

RUE St ANTOINE

MANOIR DE PRÉTOT

A HISTORIC HOME NEAR DEAUVILLE

Just a few miles west of the high life in Deauville, the Manoir de Prétot is nicely situated to enjoy both the activity of the chic resort and the tranquillity of the rural countryside. For Jacques and Floraine Poilleux, former Parisians who, with their sons, Guillaume and Christophe, have lived in this elegant 17th-century *manoir* for more than a decade, the location is eminently suitable. Jacques, a surgeon at the nearby Lisieux hospital, and Floraine, active in several local civic organizations, frequently drive over to Deauville for dinner, a dress ball at the Normandy, or perhaps a round of golf at the Club New Golf. Guillaume, a skilled horseback rider, and Christophe, who enjoys hunting, prefer to spend their leisure time traversing the woods and fields a spiritual world away from the chic center of Deauville.

Originally the home of Marie Corneille, sister of the 17th-century dramatist Pierre Corneille, the Manoir de Prétot is a beautifully preserved and restored example of the finely crafted *manoirs* constructed in the 1600s. The striking facade is sturdily built out of thick, roughly squared beams, carefully laid and spaced to support the weight of

The Manoir de Prétot, seen from the rear, right, from the front, left, and in a detail, inset right, is a classic, beautifully crafted 17th-century residence on the road between Deauville and Pont l'Évêque.

The high-ceilinged living room, left, dominated by a large carved-stone fireplace, is warmly inviting in rich tones of burgundy and butter yellow.

three stories and a steeply pitched roof. The ceramic *faîtages* that adorn the slate-shingled roof were added around 1900.

A massive oak balustrade, warmly patined and sensuously carved, accents the center hall stairway, with steps tiled in terra-cotta and bordered in oak. The entrance hall gleams with unusual black flint, or *silex,* tiles, some almost three inches thick, which date back more than three hundred years.

The decor within the Manoir de Prétot is a harmonious blend of antique and contemporary, accented with full, rich colors. Burgundy, moss green, French blue, and deep forest green each dominate a room in the house.

The gardens, including a thriving *potager,* are impeccably maintained by a full-time gardener, as well as by Floraine and Jacques. Flowers bloom abundantly throughout the property—within an old stone apple press, trimming the *potager,* and around the foundations of the former bake house, now used as a summerhouse and guest quarters.

Although a busy local road borders the property on one side, and a small railroad line, used by one or two intervillage trains a day, on another, the domain of the Manoir de Prétot, with its graveled drive, its broad lawns, and its cherry trees, remains serene, as quiet and untroubled by the commotions of life beyond the borders as it was when Pierre Corneille visited sister Marie for a few days' respite from the rigors of life in Paris.

Madame Poilleux conceived the idea for her unusual coffee-table pedestals: pewter urns filled with an assortment of bright dried flowers, right.

Beyond the Directoire table and chairs in the intimate dining room, left, the facade of a 17th-century armoire acts as a pass-through from the kitchen. Candles and pewterware top an antique buffet in a corner of the dining room, below.

A polished and patined stairway of terra-cotta tiles and oak borders rises from the house's central hallway up three stories to the small dormer rooms under the roof, left and below.

A deep forest green and the dark warm hues of old wood predominate in a cozy guest room off the second-floor landing.

In the foyer, a Napoleon III scarf with a medical theme, right, hangs against a half-timbered wall.

A former bake house on the property, left and inset right, has been restored as guest quarters and a family summerhouse. On the weekend, Jacques and Floraine Poilleux, below, enjoy puttering in the flower and vegetable gardens that make up much of their property. Fallen apples, right, dot the lawn on an early autumn day.

The carefully cultivated flowers and vegetables, above and right, groomed by a gardener and given tender loving care by Madame Poilleux, flourish in the temperate Norman climate and pay off with an abundant yield throughout the summer and fall.

PARFONDEVAL
A CHÂTEAU IN FARM COUNTRY

Broad green fields stretch out from all points around Parfondeval, a graceful 17th-century château set in the isolated farm country inland from Dieppe. The 600-acre property is several thousand miles and more than a decade away from the slick Manhattan world of young professionals where Jenifer Hyde, then an editor with *Bride's Magazine*, first met Frédéric Armand-Delille, a young French banker who was working in New York after graduating from Harvard and earning his M.B.A. in France. They married in 1977, and for two years continued their respective careers, much of that time in Brazil, where Frédéric worked for Morgan Bank. But in 1980 the future of Parfondeval, a château that had been in Frédéric's family since 1647, became uncertain. Frédéric's mother, Nolwen, had been living there with her husband, the late Sir Kenneth Clark, the renowned art historian who died in 1983. The hard work of running the large farming estate was becoming a burden, and the couple felt they could not continue alone. In a decision made over weeks of soul-searching, the young Armand-Delilles decided to give up their urban careers, or at least to put them on hold for a spell, to try out the agricultural life in rural Normandy. They would live in a château, but their existence would be dependent upon farming.

Today, after several difficult years, the farm is thriving, and so is the family. There is now a new generation of Armand-Delilles: Paul, the eldest; Clara, a year younger; and Hugues, the baby. Jenifer runs the household and does some freelance writing on the side, while Frédéric tills the fields of oats, wheat, and sugar beets, and tends the cattle.

Parfondeval, left, an elegant Louis XIII château built in the early 1600s, overlooks the woods and pasture that make up part of the 600-acre property.

The vibrant, happy family life of the Armand-Delilles has given Parfondeval, which means literally "by the bottom of the valley," an aura of vitality sadly absent from many venerable châteaus. Built around 1612, during the reign of Louis XIII, the house, of rosy brick and white limestone, has tall and elegant mullioned windows, a steeply pitched slate roof, and several beautiful *dépendances,* or outbuildings, including an orangery with a guest apartment and a pavilion where Lady Clark resides. The château has wonderful views from every window—across the wide lawns, through a long *allée* of linden trees planted by Lady Clark just after World War II, and beyond to the high fields.

The house contains rare and beautiful antiques, such as the unusual Louis XV chinoiserie panels and stone mantel in the small sitting room, and the Louis XVI *boiserie,* or woodwork, in the drawing room. A scattering of French and American children's toys, an enormous oak farm table in the vaulted basement kitchen, some slightly frayed family furniture, framed portraits, and engravings everywhere add to the air of worn gentility. Jenifer has redecorated three of the château's many rooms in airy pastels for guests visiting this tranquil and lovely area of Normandy on a long weekend's idyll in the countryside.

Two topiary ducks, below, flank a stone stairway near the main house. Framed under the archway of the former stables, right, are the Armand-Delilles with their children: Paul, left, Clara, center, and baby Hugues.

In one of the château's three guest bedrooms, a writing desk with the château's stationery sits between two windows curtained with 18th-century–style fabric recently purchased in a Paris department store, left.

Ancestral portraits, left, cover the walls of Par-fondeval, augmenting the sense of history and tradition one feels within the venerable house.

179

The main living room,
right, flooded with light
from the high French
windows on the north,
south, and east walls, is
an eclectic mélange of
gently worn furniture, a
pair of 18th-century
hand-painted folding
screens, and heirloom
objets and family me-
mentos; distinctive
Louis XIV *boiserie* em-
bellishes the walls.

In the small, intimate sitting room opening onto the front lawn, left and below left, rare Louis XV chinoiserie panels cover the walls; small statuary, porcelain lamps, and antique clocks are placed with care on the Louis XV mantel and the marble-topped tables.

The intriguing chinoiserie panel, right, here a backdrop for an 18th-century cherub, was inspired by Aesop's fables.

Jenifer Armand-Delille, a former editor at *Bride's Magazine* in New York, redecorated the luminous "honeymoon suite," left, in romantic shades of soft rose and lavender. In another guest room, above, a portrait of Queen Victoria looks down from above a sculpted 18th-century mantel.

A side entrance in the 17th-century portion of the *manoir* is sheltered by a terra-cotta roof and banked with shrubs, right.

MANOIR DE GLATIGNY
TOURGÉVILLE'S LAVISH LANDMARK

A dazzling combination of flash and class, the Manoir de Glatigny is one of the most lavish residences in Normandy. The *manoir* itself, extraordinary with its 17th-century brick-and-limestone front facade dating from the time of Louis XIII and its 15th-century half-timbered rear facade decorated with rare figurative Renaissance carvings, is a classified *monument historique*. The large property around the *manoir* includes paddocks and stables for thoroughbred horses, abundant, colorful gardens, tennis courts, two swimming pools (one indoor, complete with a built-in wall-sized aquarium, and one outdoor), and a spacious thatched-roofed pool house with two tiled rooms, one with a Jacuzzi and sauna, the other with a bar and barbecue.

Owned by a multinational investor and contractor from Paris who uses it on weekends and vacations with family and friends, this local treasure required almost a decade of restoration work and commitment to bring it to its current enviable state. Located down a narrow country lane in Tourgéville, not far from Deauville and Trouville, the Manoir de Glatigny is almost a fairy-tale realm unto itself —gamboling thoroughbreds, pristine masonry walls twined with wisteria, burbling fountains, and broad, manicured lawns sloping down to the private woodland—all secure behind high remote-control gates. This is a princely Normandy that coexists serenely with the simple hamlets and working farms just beyond the walls.

The sumptuous Manoir de Glatigny, with a 17th-century brick-and-limestone front facade, top and bottom, and a 15th-century rear facade, center, is classified as a *monument historique*.

A small guest house, right, one of several outbuildings on the property, is surrounded by its own little gardens.

Rare Renaissance carv-
ings, such as the figures
of Adam and Eve,
below left and below
center, adorn the rear
15th-century facade of
the *manoir*. Heavy
wrought-iron grilles,
bottom, protect vulner-
able ground-floor
windows. Wisteria gar-
lands the half-timbered
walls of the stables,
below right.

The unique carvings depicting royal and allegorical figures, as well as the pure 15th-century lines and timbering of the rear façade, below, were largely responsible for the classification of this *manoir* as a historic monument, an honor sought by the owners of many venerable properties.

Within the pool house are two stylish tiled rooms, one with a Jacuzzi and a sauna in azure blue, top. The grounds are decorated with flowering shrubs and terra-cotta urns, above.

One of two swimming pools, right, extends from the pool house toward the *manoir*; the other pool, to the left, and out of view in the photograph, is sheltered indoors under a long thatched roof.

VILLA LES FLOTS
AN OCEAN-VIEW FLAT IN TROUVILLE

Almost everyone who drives from Honfleur to Deauville along the Normandy Corniche, the road that runs above the coast, notices a pretty pale-pink villa down below, overlooking the beach of Trouville. The Villa Les Flots—The Waves—was once the vacation home of Gustave Eiffel, the French engineer who designed the Paris tower bearing his name. Today, this large villa has been divided into several airy, luminous apartments. A variety of apertures, from round, *oeil-de-boeuf* windows to tall French doors, allow in the profuse light, which is made more intense by reflection off the water.

The apartment on Les Flots' top floor, originally the attic, was renovated and redesigned for a young woman who works as the assistant manager at the Brasserie Les Vapeurs, the popular restaurant in Trouville. She wanted a bright, clean, contemporary look, with simple lines, to keep the spacious dimensions uncluttered. A dramatic Japanese screen dominates the living room, which also contains a Knoll table, a modular sofa, and an antique Norman commode painted pale yellow and blue,

Overlooking the beach of Trouville, left, the soft pink Villa Les Flots retains its fin de siècle charm on the outside, while the renovated interiors are strikingly modern. Set below the Corniche road among other villas, Les Flots, right, is one of the few beach residences occupied year-round.

A small stone balcony off the living room, right, offers unobstructed views of the wide beach below. The turn-of-the-century postcard shows the Villa Les Flots in its early days.

an appealing counterpoint to the modern accoutrements. A large collection of Japanese fish engravings is nicely set off against the sea-blue walls of the kitchen. The interesting fronts of the built-in kitchen cabinets were created from the old doors of a nearby villa.

Les Flots is just minutes away by car from the town of Trouville—a definite plus for the owner, who usually commutes back and forth twice a day to work at Les Vapeurs for the lunch and dinner hours. While some resorts resemble ghost towns after the summer, Trouville has a life beyond tourism and remains lively in the off-season, with a busy dockside market, animated streets, and several bustling bistros.

Out at the beach, where many houses are silent and shuttered nine or ten months a year, the Villa Les Flots stands distinct from its neighbors, not only because of its soft rosy color and architectural detail, but also because it is occupied year-round and always shows signs of life and light, visible from the road above. In the top-floor apartment, a second bedroom stands ready for weekend and vacation visits from friends who make the two-hour drive from Paris throughout the year. From the balcony, guests can watch the bathers and joggers on the broad beach below. Some actually take to the chilly waters, but most prefer to remain observers, sunning themselves for an hour or two before heading into town for shopping or dinner and a chance to chat with their hostess across the bar or from behind platters heaped with local *fruits de mer*.

A variety of apertures, above right, above far right, and far right, illuminate the airy, modern interior of this *belle époque* residence built in 1870. Standing at the raised entrance of Les Flots, right, is the owner of the top-floor flat.

Carved out of space that was once the villa's attic, the living room, right, is bright and airy with a variety of windows, cathedral ceilings, and high, asymmetrical walls.

Next to a bedroom that parallels the living room, right, and below right, an unusual collection of antique Japanese fish engravings reflects the villa's maritime setting. The living room's inspiration is resolutely modern, with some Knoll furnishings, a sisal rug, and dramatic Japanese accents.

A white flowered pathway leads to the door of the Levêques' historic 16th-century manor house near Lisieux, right, built during the reign of François I. Among the many fine architectural features of the Manoir d'Aubichon are the carved details on exterior beams, below.

MANOIR D'AUBICHON

A 16TH-CENTURY TREASURE NEAR LISIEUX

As president of the Association "Le Pays d'Auge," Dr. Claude Levêque is deeply involved with preserving and promoting the architectural, artistic, and cultural heritage of his region. Perhaps inspiring his avocation, or perhaps because of it, his own home, the 16th-century Manoir d'Aubichon, is one of the fine and rare antique manor houses that make up the rich architectural patrimony of this area.

Dr. Levêque traces the origins of the house, which has been in his family for over forty years, to sometime between 1505 and 1535, pointing to a sculpted coat of arms on the facade that represents Cardinal Jean IV le Veneur, a nobleman who was bishop of Lisieux during those years. Painstakingly restored over two decades, the house is a labor of love for Dr. Levêque and his wife, Yvonne. Much of the painted woodwork inside, including the trompe l'oeil walls of the *bibliothèque* and doors copied from the Musée Carnavalet in Paris, was done by Dr. Levêque himself.

Dr. Claude Levêque and his wife, Yvonne, above, restored their house slowly over more than twenty years. Up the path from the manoir, atop a small incline, the summerhouse is positioned to catch cooling breezes.

The *manoir* is a solidly built rectangular dwelling set full in the countryside on the outskirts of Lisieux in the Orbiquet River valley. An extremely pure example of 16th-century design, the facade has narrow vertical clay-filled timberwork, sculpted supporting beams, decorative polychrome coats of arms, and mullioned windows. One very rare quality of the Manoir d'Aubichon is that there are still traces of the ocher-red paint that once covered the *colombage*, the wood of the timbered facade. (It comes as a surprise to many people that the original timbered facades of some antique manor houses, today left natural or stained a deep brown, were once multicolored.) The *manoir* is constructed around four massive limestone fireplaces, which feed into one large central chimney.

Outside, in the grounds, a white-flowered pathway landscaped by the Levêques leads up to a restored granary, now used as a summerhouse and game room. Nearby, cows on a neighboring property graze peacefully under the apple trees. The Manoir d'Aubichon, as remote and tranquil today as it was four hundred years ago, reflects one couple's pride and passion in their region and their heritage. Not surprisingly, the Levêques' property is a classified *monument historique*.

The *café au lait* hue of the living room, left, is a warm neutral background for the antique tapestries, oriental rugs, and hand-painted trompe l'oeil *bibliothèque* that personalize the room. Dr. Levêque created the *bibliothèque* himself, painting books on the glass cabinet doors to hide the television within.

The Levêques chose a soft gray for the walls of the dining room, right, to harmonize with the stones of the period fireplace.

At one end of the living room, right, Madame Levêque's collection of romantic *objets* catches the afternoon sun.

An oriental rug adds
visual warmth to Dr.
Levêque's stone-walled
study on the second
floor, above, while a
broad fireplace takes
the chill off in cool
weather.

The decor of the sum-
merhouse, right, is
comfortable and unpre-
tentious, featuring
masses of cotton print
pillows, framed posters,
and painted garden
furniture.

CHEZ LES BAZIRES

A RESTAURATEUR'S VICTORIAN RETREAT

When Martine and Gérard Bazire found their comfortable 19th-century brick house in the town of Touques, it was in deplorable condition. *"Toute rude!"* recalls Martine. "It was filthy with chicken droppings everywhere inside, and the walls and floors were in terrible shape." But looking beyond the dismal state of the interior, and an unkempt yard, the Bazires saw that the building and property had vast potential, and decided to buy it. In renovating the house from top to bottom, Martine used as many old materials as she could find locally —original 19th-century tiles, beams from razed houses, and antique fixtures.

Martine Bazire stands with her sons, Gregory, left, and Romain, center, at the top of the steps that overlook the backyard, left. The Bazire home, right, squarely proportioned and constructed of rose and cream brick, is typical of many solid bourgeois houses built in Normandy during the mid- to late 1800s.

Built in 1869 of rose- and cream-colored brick, the house has a romantic Victorian air, enhanced within by potted palms, swags of lace and velvet at the windows, English floral-print wallpaper, tinted blown-glass lamps, and walls hung with densely grouped watercolors or framed miniatures. The surrounding gardens have been carefully cultivated by Martine, who has an inspired green thumb. Her deeply perfumed roses grow in profusion, and the vegetables in the *potager* have been known to reach prize-winning proportions.

The Bazires both work long hours in their popular restaurant, the Brasserie Les Vapeurs in nearby Trouville. Originally in the food-service business in Paris, where they ran a club dining room, they bought Les Vapeurs several years ago when a friend told them that the venerable brasserie, opened in 1927, was up for sale. Even the Bazires' young sons pitch in at the lively eatery on weekends in exchange for their weekly allowance. Gregory, the older boy, fetches bottles of wine for the waiters, and little Romain helps wash the coffee cups one hour a day. In their off-hours the boys ride their bikes, play ball in the yard at home, or finish their schoolwork, while Gérard is off on one of several athletic pursuits and Martine retreats to the restful beauty of her gardens.

A lavish heirloom lace curtain, left, filters light into the Bazires' intimate living room, which is imbued with a sense of *temps perdu*.

The intensely Victorian living room, designed like a cozy sitting room, strongly evokes the style of the late 1800s, with its velvet settee, curtain swags, draped shawls, potted palms, floral wallpaper, and clustered collections of watercolors and etchings on the walls.

212

"On Sunday night," Martine Bazire relates, "friends come to have coffee here in front of the fire before they return to Paris." Densely accessorized yet not overwhelming, the living room, right, has a *sympathique* quality that keeps visitors lingering long after they should have set off *en route*.

Aligned doorways give a clear perspective from the collectible-filled kitchen, foreground left, through the foyer and into the living room.

A long, rustic, 19th-century farm table placed by a kitchen window serves as the dining table, left.

A raised central fireplace next to the tile-backed stove, above, is the kitchen's warm and glowing heart.

Ingredients of this quintessential country kitchen include faience tiles, exposed beams, an array of shining copper pots, antique cupboards laden with old crockery, and, here and there, whimsical family memorabilia. Blue burlap, enhancing the kitchen's rustic quality, covers the walls between beams.

217

The artfully old-fashioned bathroom, above, in fin de siècle shades of mauve and lavender, has a floral theme that is carried through from the hand-painted tiles and the fresh-cut bouquets to the petal-shaped sconces on the wall.

The delicate lace coverlet, the lace throw pillows stitched by Martine's grandmother, the indigo-ground floral wallpaper, and the collection of miniatures above the brass bed combine to create the master bedroom's romantic 19th-century ambience, right. "Another key," says Martine, "is that nothing is exactly symmetrical."

Sunlight and hints of color from the front gardens filter through the intricately cut and stitched flowers of the bedroom's antique lace-and-linen curtains, left. A fall afternoon's harvest, gathered from Martine Bazire's flourishing *potager,* forms a brilliant, dewy still life on the backyard picnic table, right.

MOULIN DE FALAISE

A WATER-MILL HOME IN THE VAL D'ANTE

Sheltered by a four-hundred-year-old chestnut tree, this rock-solid *moulin à eau,* or water mill, built alongside a riverbank, enjoys a unique setting. The famous ramparts of the fortified town of Falaise soar skyward only a few steps away, yet the property itself, facing a placid pond and thick with lofty oaks and poplars, seems to be lost deep in the countryside.

Several years ago a local couple, both of whom are doctors in Falaise as well as connoisseurs of French antiques, purchased the house because of its location (just five minutes from town), its history, and its rural ambience. The house comprises many parts; the earliest—the actual mill housing—dates from the 15th century, with other sections added from the 16th to the 18th centuries. Constructed of *pierre de Caen,* or limestone, the mill provided power for the town's tanneries and hatters, industries important to the region from the 17th century until almost 1900. Today, the ancient wooden waterwheel long gone, the mill no longer functions. But the venerable house, which had remained in the same family for almost five hundred years before it was bought by the current owners in the late 1970s, is sound enough to face another half-millenium with equanimity.

Lights pierce the austere stone facade of the 15th-century water-mill home in Falaise, left. In a small bedroom used as a game room, right, a portrait of Marie-Antoinette hangs above a painted Louis XVI fauteuil; the black cord around her neck indicates that she has been guillotined. Lavish floral-print Braquenier fabric covers the walls.

The oldest portion of the house is the original 15th-century mill-housing which today is the spacious beamed kitchen, left. An early 19th-century Norman armoire holding faience and crockery faces a round 19th-century dining table in walnut.

In one corner of the kitchen, left, a collection of 19th-century faience is displayed above a sculpted 17th-century fireplace. Dozing in the armchair by the fire is Anaïs, the family's pet greyhound.

A painted and elegantly carved fauteuil, above, one of a pair in the living room, has a tapestry seat stitched at the turn of the 19th century near Dieppe. An 18th-century tapestry frame from Bayeux, left, with handsome ironwork detailing, stands at an angle before one of the wide living room windows.

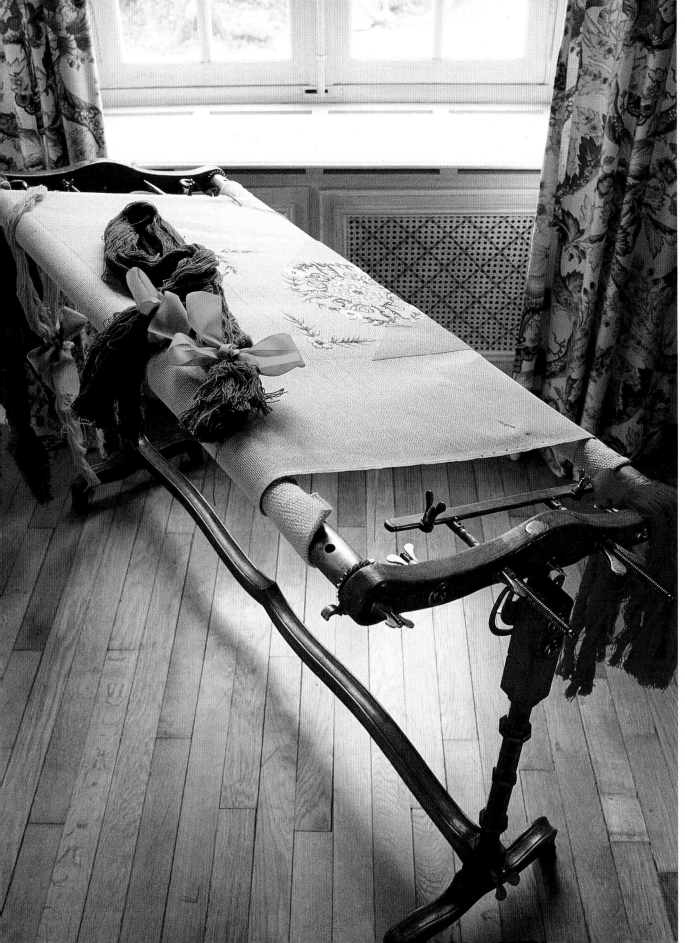

Seventeenth-century woodwork and dramatic floral fabric by Braquenier embellish the master alcove-bedroom, right. In the foreground is a painted and upholstered 17th-century *lit de repos,* or daybed.

PORTFOLIO

A GUIDE TO SHOPPING AND STAYING IN NORMANDY

Regional antiques and products are perhaps the finest souvenirs you can bring back from a visit to one of France's distinctive provinces. Our Portfolio is a guide to sources for the best antiques and gourmet products that Normandy has to offer. It is also a travel guide, with suggestions for what to see, where to eat, and where to stay throughout the province—all the essentials, apart from guaranteed sunshine, for a happy, comfortable, and fulfilling trip. *Bon voyage en Normandie!*

ANTIQUES

SEINE-MARITIME

In this antique-rich region, *antiquaires,* or antiques dealers, specialize in high-quality traditional Norman oak furniture: sculpted armoires, buffets, grandfather clocks from Saint-Nicolas-d'Aliermont, and farm tables. One can also find 17th- and 18th-century faience from Rouen, antique pottery cider pitchers and mugs, carved ivories from Dieppe, and nautical collectibles. Dealers with an asterisk after their names are the major *antiquaires* in town.

DIEPPE (postal code 76200)

Abraham 55 quai Henri-IV. Tel. 35 84 28 46.

Chineurs (Les) 3 rue des Bains. Tel. 35 84 26 46.

Couvert 22 rue de la Barre. Tel. 35 84 47 20. *

Dantec 2 rue Denys. Tel. 35 82 23 76. *

Gaffe 4 rue Villatte. Tel. 35 84 17 06. *

Kotarba 22 rue de la Barre. Tel. 35 84 00 90. *

Laurent 8 rue de l'Oranger. *

Plessis 21 quai Henri-IV. Tel. 35 82 69 39.

Sutton 29 rue des Bains. Tel. 35 84 86 72.

Vauquelin (Glie) 4 rue Vauquelin. Tel. 35 84 31 78. *

Vergnory 14 chemin du Golf. Tel. 35 82 56 22.

FÉCAMP (postal code 76400)

Brocante 76 quai Berigny.

Grenier à Sel 34 boulevard de la République. Tel. 35 27 31 51.

ROUEN (postal code 76000)

Adam T'Elle (L') 47 rue Damiette. Tel. 35 07 71 75. *

Albuquerque 7 & 9 rue des Bonnetiers. Tel. 35 88 00 65.

Angue 210 rue Martainville. Tel. 35 70 51 90. *

Antiquités Rive Gauche (Resse) 51 bis rue Pavée. Tel. 35 72 21 22. *

Arizzoli 83 rue d'Amiens. Tel. 35 71 60 37.

Bateau Lavoir (Le). 174 rue Eau-de-Robec. Tel. 35 07 43 00, 79 10 02. *

Baudeu rue Croix-de-Fer. Tel. 35 89 38 62.

Bayeul 154 rue Eau-de-Robec. Tel. 35 98 13 33.

Belliard 7 rue Damiette. Tel. 35 98 46 29. *

Bertrán (E.) 110 rue Molière. Tel. 35 70 79 96. *

Bertrán (M.) 108 rue Molière. Tel. 35 98 24 06. *

Bigot-Commenchal 20b–42 rue St.-Romain. Tel. 35 98 54 40, 70 36 36.

Boisnard 18 rue Thiers. Tel. 35 71 57 44. *

Brument 14 rue Écuyère. Tel. 35 70 37 39. *

Carpentier 26 rue St.-Romain. *

Charlotte 41 rue Beauvoisine. Tel. 35 98 70 88.

Chasset 12 rue Croix-de-Fer. Tel. 35 70 59 97.

Chemin 18–20 rue Damiette. Tel. 35 98 41 11.

Cleon (A.) 158 rue Eau-de-Robec. Tel. 35 70 83 82.

Cleon (M.) 164 rue Eau-de-Robec. Tel. 35 88 63 16. *

Comptoir Rouennais 4 place de la Pucelle. Tel. 35 89 80 84. *

Comptoir St.-Georges 35 rue aux Juifs. Tel. 35 89 59 99. *

Dédicaces 11 rue Alain-Blanchard. Tel. 35 71 10 13.

Delacroix 3 rue Percière. Tel. 35 71 84 35.

Deraisin 9 rue Damiette.
Tel. 35 88 92 17. *
Dezandre 228 rue Martainville.
Tel. 35 07 53 05. *
Du Mesnil Gaillard 54 rue des Bons-Enfants.
Tel. 35 71 05 97. *
Fernette 11 place Barthélémy.
Tel. 35 70 75 62.
Foubert 46 rue Damiette.
Garnier 11 rue Damiette.
Tel. 35 88 66 85.
Grenier Michel (Au) 9 rue Damiette.
Tel. 35 66 17 18.
Grindel 1–3 rue Croix-de-Fer/Frantel.
Tel. 35 98 08 40.
Gruson 9 rue Damiette.
Tel. 35 88 55 81.

Hesse 194 rue Eau-de-Robec.
Tel. 35 98 00 30. *
Insolite 29 rue Damiette.
Tel. 35 07 48 49. *
Labiche 10 rue Damiette.
Tel. 35 89 95 75.
Larbi 10 rue des Augustins. *
Lavalley 35 rue Damiette.
Tel. 35 88 16 10. *
Lefaux 64 bis rue de Fontenelle.
Tel. 35 88 80 69.
Le Pennec 27 rue Damiette.
Tel. 35 71 65 05. *
Lespinasse (Glle) 220 rue Martainville.
Tel. 35 89 38 15.
Brocante (M. R.) 41 rue St.-Gervais.
Tel. 35 70 05 87.
Magne 20 rue de l'Hôpital.
Tel. 35 88 76 31. *
Maine 112 rue Malpalu.
Tel. 35 71 75 75.
Malejac 8 rue Damiette.
Tel. 35 71 45 62.
Maréchal 239 rue Eau-de-Robec.
Tel. 35 88 05 02. *
Maurice 9 rue Damiette.
Tel. 35 71 56 05.
Mauve et Goût 15 rue de l'École.
Tel. 35 89 25 33.
Metais 2 place Barthélémy.
Tel. 35 70 94 33. *
Morisse 170 rue Eau-de-Robec.
Tel. 35 07 44 57. *
Nautilus 59 rue de la République.
Tel. 35 89 69 23.
Paradis de l'Ancien (Au) 87–60 rue Thier.
Tel. 35 89 44 24. *
Pillet (Jean-François) 3 place Barthélémy.
Tel. 35 07 44 10. *
Pivain 54 rue Damiette.
Tel. 35 70 21 32. *
Plachot 219 rue Eau-de-Robec.
Tel. 35 07 13 80. *
Planage 41 rue Damiette. *
Popelin 20 rue St.-Romain.
Tel. 35 71 35 06.
Poulingue 4 place Barthélémy.
Tel. 35 98 09 56.
Poulingue 9 rue Damiette.
Tel. 35 88 21 74. *
Prezelin 49 rue d'Amiens.
Tel. 35 98 60 32.
Regnier 45 rue Damiette.
Tel. 35 07 63 95.

Rouen-Numismatique 37 quai du Havre.
Tel. 35 07 03 72.
St.-Maclou-Antic 178 rue Martainville.
Tel. 35 89 52 61, 98 36 31. *
Schlomka 22 rue St.-Romain.
Segas 3 rue d'Écosse.
Tel. 35 70 02 52. *
Serventon 23 rue Damiette.
Tel. 35 89 89 89. *
Tellier (Galerie) 15 rue St.-Denis.
Tel. 35 98 18 18. *
Testu-Vedie 60 rue St.-Romain.
Tel. 35 71 59 66.
Tetelin (Max) 14 rue St.-Romain.
Tel. 35 71 43 33. *
Tourraton 13 rue Damiette.
Tel. 35 98 47 42. *
Vetu (P.) 64 rue St.-Romain.
Tel. 35 89 35 06.

VARENGEVILLE (postal code 76119)

Guiho route de Ste.-Marguerite.
Tel. 35 85 11 36. *
Patchworks Sabine du Tertre, les maisons.
Tel. 35 85 14 64. *
(new quilts from rare antique fabrics)

EURE

In the Eure one can find oak armoires, buffets, and commodes that are somewhat sober and reserved, less lushly carved and ostentatious than in other regions. Dealers also carry antique copperware, 19th-century porcelain, regional jewelry, and paintings from the 18th and 19th centuries.

CONCHES (postal code 27190)

Bagland 1 route Ste.-Marguerite.
Tel. 32 30 21 14. *
Thoumyre 2 rue St.-Étienne.
Tel. 32 30 04 38.

ÉVREUX (postal code 27000)

Bresson 76 rue de Pannette.
Tel. 32 38 77 31.
Duchemin 3 rue Charles-Corbeau.
Tel. 32 33 06 86. *
Floreal 41 rue de la Harpe.
Tel. 32 33 22 33.

Hier et Aujourd'hui 6 avenue Aristide-Briand.
Tel. 32 39 70 76.
Leroux 42 rue St.-Louis.
Tel. 32 39 47 27.
Temps Perdus (Aux) 6 avenue Aristide-Briand.

VERNEUIL-SUR-AVRE (postal code 27130)

Antiquités Saint-Martin R. N. 12.
Tel. 32 32 19 88. *
Antiquités Subek 940 598 rue de la Madeleine.
Tel. 32 32 32 45.

ORNE

Antiquaires in the Orne offer, in addition to a range of Norman furniture that includes glass-doored chest-on-chests, farm tables, and lightly sculpted oak armoires, a selection of antique pottery and kitchen utensils, jewelry, and lace and shawls from Alençon.

BAGNOLES-DE-L'ORNE (postal code 61140)

Ambrosi 4 place de la République. Tel. 33 30 05 91. *

DOMFRONT (postal code 61700)

Beauchef 16 place Notre-Dame.
Tel. 33 66 95 85. *

Oubliette (L') 54 rue Dr. Barrabé.
Tel. 33 38 91 06. *

FLERS (postal code 61100)

Atelier (L') 24 rue de la Boule.
Tel. 33 65 26 83.

Chanu route de Caen-Rainette.
Tel. 33 65 08 20.

Havas 15 rue Victor-Hugo.
Tel. 33 65 31 09. *

PIN-AU-HARAS (Le) (postal code 61310)

Guerin-Wallner à la Tête-au-Loup.
Tel. 33 67 92 21.

Sanchez
Tel. 33 67 41 30.

CALVADOS

Traditional sculpted oak armoires, buffets, linen chests, étagères, and grandfather clocks in the "demoiselle" style are among the antiques available from dealers in Calvados. One also finds Bayeux porcelain, Rouen faience, butter molds, pewter or pottery cider pitchers, painted hope chests, and laces from Caen and Bayeux.

BAYEUX (postal code 14400)

Brocante du Bessin 8 rue St.-Martin.
Tel. 31 92 14 11.

Eudier 94 rue des Bouchers.
Tel. 31 92 88 94. *

Lanterne (La) 1 rue des Chanoines.
Tel. 31 92 14 54.

Lecaudey 73 rue St.-Malo.
Tel. 31 92 07 05.

Mandarine (La) 16 Parvis de la Cathédrale.
Tel. 31 92 71 77.

Vasseur Parvis de la Cathédrale.
Tel. 31 80 13 77.

BREUIL-EN-AUGE (Le) (postal code 14360)

Geffroy route Pont-l'Évêque-Lisieux.
Tel. 31 64 75 20.

CAEN (postal code 14000)

Alerini 9 rue des Croisiers.
Tel. 31 85 57 50.

Antiquités Saint-Laurent 10 rue St.-Laurent.
Tel. 31 86 36 05. *

Archive (L') 13 rue Écuyère.
Tel. 31 85 12 56, 86 27 69.

Basnier 40 rue Écuyère.
Tel. 31 85 36 58. *

Belle Époque (La) 66–68 rue St.-Jean.
Tel. 31 85 63 37.

Blondel 10 bis rue Froide.
Tel. 31 86 61 40.

Boblin 80 avenue Henry-Chéron.
Tel. 31 73 27 91.

Boîte à Livres (La) 33 rue des Teinturiers.
Tel. 31 85 59 19. *

Bouet 6 rue Froide.
Tel. 31 85 51 80.

Brillet 15 rue des Croisiers.
Tel. 31 86 59 64.

Brocante Caennaise (La) 68 bis rue Falaise.
Tel. 31 52 00 63.

Brune 19 rue Écuyère.
Tel. 31 85 48 77. *

Caen-Numisma 34 bis rue de Bras.
Tel. 31 86 43 38. *

Caen-Philatélie 97 rue St.-Jean.
Tel. 31 86 04 35. *

Cherche Hier (Au) 19 rue des Teinturiers.
Tel. 31 85 60 76.

Choses Recherchées (Aux) 13 rue Écuyère.
Tel. 31 86 49 23.

Comptoir St.-Georges 50 avenue de la Libération.
Tel. 31 43 60 60. *

Dufford 10 rue Laumonnier.
Tel. 31 94 64 41. *

Dumoussaud-Morel 32 rue Écuyère.
Tel. 31 86 62 03. *

Dumoussaud 17 rue Écuyère.
Tel. 31 85 48 83. *

Fontaine-Sement 45 bis rue Écuyère.
Tel. 31 85 41 67. *

Fragments 11 rue St.-Laurent.
Tel. 31 86 29 16.

Godey 25 rue Écuyère.
Tel. 31 86 48 06. *

Gonet 50 rue Écuyère.
Tel. 31 85 72 67. *

Jean-Louis Antiquités 16 rue Écuyère.
Tel. 31 86 61 60. *

Le Brun 26 rue d'Authie.
Tel. 31 73 04 23.

Magasin l'Écu 1 rue de la Miséricorde.
Tel. 31 50 02 32. *

Marie 9 bis rue du Québec.
Tel. 31 74 44 54.

Marnoni 17 rue Écuyère.
Tel. 31 85 54 05. *

Reine Mathilde (R. Le Ber) 47 rue St.-Jean.
Tel. 31 85 45 52. *

Roxane's Antiques 2 bis rue aux Fromages.
Tel. 31 86 66 51.

Salaun 1 rue de l'Engarrene.
Tel. 31 85 30 03. *

Simeon Daniel, Presse Ancienne 59 rue des Jacobins.
Tel. 31 86 66 88. *

Souvenirs d'Antan 6 avenue du 6-Juin.
Tel. 31 86 88 68.

Temps Retrouvé (Le) 34 rue Écuyère.
Tel. 31 86 62 03. *

Theet 40 rue Écuyère.
Tel. 31 85 72 88.

Tixier (Galerie Didier) 12 rue Gémar.
Tel. 31 50 24 60. *

Toulorge 14 rue Froide.
Tel. 31 86 14 65.

Vautier 38 rue Écuyère.
Tel. 31 85 57 75. *

DEAUVILLE (postal code 14800)

Aurore 79 rue du Général Leclerc.
Tel. 31 88 52 07.

Modestie 34 rue Gambetta.
Tel. 31 98 11 96.

O'Deauville 9 rue Gontaut Biron.
Tel. 31 88 62 21.

O'Sodexmao 2 rue Gontaut Biron.
Tel. 31 88 21 00.

Salle des Ventes (auction rooms) 16 rue du Général-Leclerc.
Tel. 31 88 21 92.
Sundays, 10:00–12:00 and 2:00–7:00.

HONFLEUR (postal code 14600)

Antiquaire de la Côte de Grâce (L') 5 Ancienne route de Trouville.
Tel. 31 89 05 21. *

Bérthelon 22 rue de la Ville.
Tel. 31 89 28 37.

Blanpain 10 rue des Lingots.
Tel. 31 89 17 13.

Bourdon 29 rue des Logettes.
Tel. 31 89 04 35.

Brocanterie (La) 11 cours des Fossés.
Tel. 31 89 05 36.

Doucet 22 place Hamelin.

Gorzkowski, "La Brocanterie" 11 cours des Fossés.
Tel. 31 89 05 38. *

Griffoul 14 rue de l'Homme-de-Bois.
Tel. 31 89 29 54. *

Hamelin (Glle) 32 place Hamelin.
Tel. 31 98 88 73. *

Lebey 20 rue des Lingots. *

Nounouche 1 rue du Puits.
Tel. 31 89 46 53.

Panossian 2 rue Brûlée.
Tel. 31 98 88 62.

Renouf 13 rue des Logettes.
Tel. 31 89 21 97. *

Rohaut 27 rue des Logettes.
Tel. 31 89 31 04. *

LISIEUX (postal code 14100)

Bouquerel 21 quai des Remparts.
  Tel. 31 31 63 06.

Brocante St.-Clair route de Caen et rue de Falaise.
  Tel. 31 31 37 22.

Cage Ouverte (La) 27 place de la République.
  Tel. 31 62 15 59.

Chereau 7 boulevard Ste.-Anne.
  Tel. 31 62 66 32. *

Hervieu 5 place du Général-de-Gaulle.
  Tel. 31 62 18 79. *

Salle des Affaires 70 avenue Victor-Hugo.
  Tel. 31 31 59 71.

VIRE (postal code 14500)

Vilars Face à l'Hôpital, 7 rue Émile-Desvaux.
  Tel. 31 68 07 94. *

MANCHE

In the Manche, *antiquaires* carry fine traditional Norman furniture in oak, such as sculpted armoires, sometimes embellished with gleaming copperware, chest-on-chests with solid or glassed-in cabinet doors, and linen chests. Dealers also offer Bayeux porcelain, pewter measuring pitchers, lace headdresses, and a range of old copperware from Villedieu-les-Poêles: casseroles, milk pitchers, sauté pans, and large fish steamers.

AVRANCHES (postal code 50300)

Cheminais 14 rue des Chapeliers.
  Tel. 33 58 20 66.

Dodier 1 rue de Bremesnil.
  Tel. 33 58 05 81.

Gervais (G.) 13 boulevard du Luxembourg.
  Tel. 33 58 35 16.

Gervais au Perroquet Vert 38 rue de la Constitution.
  Tel. 33 58 02 54. *

Métairie (La) 71 rue Commandant-Bindel.
  Tel. 33 58 43 08. *

Pinson 2 place Angot.
  Tel. 33 58 47 62.

Pouquet 80 rue de la Constitution.
  Tel. 33 58 14 55.

Therin boulevard Léon-Jozeau Marigné.
  Tel. 33 58 07 82.

Vauborel (De) 176 rue de la Liberté.
  Tel. 33 58 00 64.

CHERBOURG (postal code 50100)

Antiquités Allix 15 rue Notre Dame.
  Tel. 33 93 63 00.

Denis 181 avenue de Paris.
  Tel. 33 44 15 31. *

Drieu la Rochelle 51 rue au Blé.
  Tel. 33 53 45 04. *

Fontanet 18 rue au Fourdray.
  Tel. 33 53 25 69.

Gourdelier 52 rue Tour-Carré.
  Tel. 33 53 21 99. *

Lerouxel 2 rue de l'Union.
  Tel. 33 53 49 96.

COUTANCES (postal code 50200)

Langelier Manoir de Saussey, Saussey.
Tel. 33 45 19 65.

SAINT-LÔ (postal code 50000)

Ancestrale (L') 587 boulevard de la Dollée.
Tel. 33 57 24 13.

SAINT-QUENTIN-SUR L'HOMME (postal code 50220)

Cherpitel L'Isle Manière.
Tel. 33 58 38 73.

VALOGNES (Postal code 50700)

Campain 6 rue Barbey d'Aurevilly.
Tel. 33 40 00 23.

Duchemin 35 rue Henri-Cornat.
Tel. 33 40 08 94.

Duteurtre 40 bis rue de la Poterie.
Tel. 33 40 34 16.

Lefebvre 29 rue Henri-Cornat.
Tel. 33 40 19 94. *

VILLEDIEU-LES-POÊLES (postal code 50800)

E. Mervy 39 rue Docteur Havard.
Tel. 33 51 18 51.
48 rue du Pont Chignon.
Tel. 33 90 00 89.

ANTIQUES FAIRS AND MARKETS

For precise dates, contact the Bureau de Tourisme in each town, or the French National Tourist Office, 630 Fifth Avenue, New York, NY 10019.

Cabourg: Foire aux Antiquités (antiques fair), Cour de la Mairie, week of August 15.

Caen: Flea Market on the Petite Place, rue du Vaugueux, first Saturday of every month. Salon des Antiquaires, Parc des Expositions, late spring.

Deauville: Salle des Ventes (auction rooms), 16 rue du Général-Leclerc, Sundays, 10 A.M. to noon, 2 P.M. to 7 P.M.

Lisieux: Salon de l'Objet Ancien et Multi-Collections, Parc des Expositions, late April or early May.

Rouen: Flea Market, Clos Saint Marc, Saturdays and Sundays.
Flea Market, place des Emmures, Thursdays.
Flea Market, rue Eau-de-Robec, first Wednesday of every month.
Salon des Antiquaires, Halle aux Toiles, end of April.
Salon National des Antiquaires, Parc des Expositions, mid-autumn.

FESTIVALS, FAIRS, AND ANNUAL EVENTS

MARCH

Mortagne-au-Perche: Foire au Boudin (Sausage Fair), last weekend of March.

APRIL

Deauville, Trouville: Easter festivals.

Rouen: International Motor Boat Races, April 30, May 1.

MAY

Cabourg: Flower show.

Beuvron-en-Auge: Geranium Festival, Place de la Halle, end of May.

Caen: Tripes à la Mode de Caen Competition.

Lisieux: Agricultural fair, end of May.

Rouen: Joan of Arc Festival, end of May.

Vernon: Foire aux Cerises (Cherry Fair), last weekend in May.

JUNE

Honfleur: Seamen's Festival (Blessing of the Sea), Whitsunday and Monday.

Sainte-Mère-Église and Sainte-Marine-du-Pont: D-Day commemoration at Utah Beach, June 5 and 6.

Harcourt: Horse show, end of June.

Villedieu-les-Poêles: Le Grand Sacré (The Great Rite), Procession of the Knights of Malta, second or third Sunday in June, every four years (1987, 1991, 1995 . . .)

Cabourg: Summer festivals.

Carrouges: Music festival in castle park, June, July, August.

JULY

Camembert: Fête du Camembert (Camembert Festival), last Sunday in July.

Le Havre: International regatta.

La Hage-de-Routot: Saint Clair Fireworks and Bonfire, July 16.

Granville: Pardon of the Corporations of the Sea, open-air mass and torchlight procession, last Sunday in July.

AUGUST

Cabourg: International tennis tournament, first two weeks in August.

Deauville: Grand Prix horse-racing. Yearling sales, end of August.

Sainte-Marguerite: Fishing competition, second Sunday in August.

SEPTEMBER

Cabourg: Horse show, first Saturday and Sunday in September.

Haras-du-Pin: Festival of Horse and Carriage, first Sunday in September, second Sunday in October.

Lessay: Foire St. Croix, or Holy Cross Fair, the largest and most traditional fair in Normandy, September 9–12.

Caen: Agricultural fair, last four days in September.

Caudebec-en-Caux: Cider festival, last Sunday in September of even years.

Alençon: Stock-raising festival, late September, early October.

Deauville: American Film Festival, one week in September.

OCTOBER

La Ferté-Macé: Journées Mycologiques (mushroom-hunting days), middle of October.

Vire: Foie gras fair, place du Champs Foire, end of October, early November.

Étoury: Animal fair, place du Marché, end of October.

NOVEMBER

Dieppe: Foire aux Harengs (Herring Fair), first weekend in November.

Deauville: Yearling sales, mid-November, early December.

DECEMBER

Évreux: Foire Saint-Nicholas (Saint Nicholas Day Fair), December 6.

REGIONAL SPECIALTIES: FRESH FROM THE PRODUCERS

For brochures on visiting cheese producers and cider and Calvados producers ("La Route du Fromage" and "La Route du Cidre," both available in English), write to the Bureau du Tourisme du Calvados, Place du Canada, 14000 Caen, France.

CIDER AND CALVADOS

Beuvron-en-Auge: Marcel David. Manoir du Sens, between the village of Beuvron and La-Chapelle-de-Clermont. Tel. 31 79 23 05. Will mail-order.

Grandouet: Roger Giard. On Route D85A, between Montreuil-en-Auge and the Église de Grandouet. Tel. 31 63 02 40.

Victot-Pontfol: Étienne Dupont. On the D16 road, about one mile from the Carrefour-Saint-Jean. Tel. 31 63 03 75. Will mail-order.

CHEESES

Boissey: Denis Thebault, "La Houssaye." Tel. 31 20 64 00. Daily except Saturday and Sunday.

Camembert: Robert Durant, "La Heronnière." Tel. 33 39 08 08. Open daily.

Livarot: Bernard Graindorge. Tel. 31 63 50 02. Fromagerie du Conservatoire. 16 rue Levesque. Tel. 31 63 45 96. Cheese tasting, see cheeses made. Daily except Monday and Tuesday.

Notre Dame de Fresnay: Fromagerie de Fresnay. Tel. 31 20 63 34. Daily except Saturday and Sunday.

PASTRY AND CHOCOLATE SHOPS

Caen: Yves Pomarede, "Chocolaterie Hotot." Rue St.-Pierre.

Deauville: G. Le Monnier, pâtissier. 20 place du Morny.

Domfront: A. Laniepce, pâtissier. 4 rue de la République.

Fécamp: L. P. Porée, pâtissier. 5 rue A. P. Leroux.

Rouen: M. Mesrouze, pâtissier-chocolatier, 38 rue Armand-Carrel.
J. P. Coupel, pâtissier, 108 rue St.-Julien.

Verneuil-sur-Avre: J. N. Le Paroux, "Aux Délices de la Tour." 140 place de la Madeleine.

Deauville: B. Lebreton. 57 bis rue Désiré-le-Hoc.

Évreux: J. Morel, "Charcuterie Fine, Cuisine." Centre Commercial Principal de la Madeleine.

Vire: Andouille d'Amandes. 5 rue Calvados.

POISSONNERIES (fish markets)

Caen: Le Grand Large. Avenue du 6-Juin.
La Triperie d'Or. 16 rue St.-Jean.

Trouville: Daily fish market with many individual stands. Boulevard F. Moureaux.

STRAWBERRIES, RASPBERRIES, PEARS, APPLES (seasonally)

La Rivière Saint-Sauveur: Didier Allaume. About one mile east of Honfleur on the D580 road. Daily.

WEEKLY MARKETS (where regional products are colorfully displayed and sold at small stands)

Alençon: Saturday morning.

Bagnoles-de-l'Orne: Saturday morning.

Caen: daily, except Monday.

Deauville: daily in season.

Dives-sur-mer: Saturday morning.

Honfleur: Saturday morning.

Lisieux: Saturday morning.

L'Aigle: Tuesdays.

Livarot: Thursday morning.

Orbec: Saturday morning.

Rouen: daily, except Monday.

Trouville: Wednesday and Saturday mornings.

Villedieu-les-Poêles: Tuesday mornings.

Vimoutiers: Monday morning.

Yvetot: Wednesday morning.

VISITING NORMANDY

WHERE TO STAY

All of these inns have restaurants that welcome guests for both lunch and dinner. Whether you are planning to go just for a meal or for an overnight stay, reservations are recommended. The simple courtesy is appreciated by the innkeepers. You will also be assured that the chef will be in the kitchen on a given day or that a room that fits your needs will be available.

Auberge de l'Abbaye. 27800 Le Bec Hellouin.
Tel. 32 44 86 02. A rambling 18th-century village inn with a rustic dining room, good food, and modest prices.

Château d'Audrieu. 14250 Audrieu par Tilly-sur-Seulles. Tel. 31 80 21 52. A luxurious château-hotel with beautiful grounds, a swimming pool, and some of the finest cuisine in Normandy.

Ferme Saint-Simeon. 14600 Honfleur. Tel. 31 89 23 61. A distinguished and stunning slate-covered inn, once frequented by the impressionist painters Monet, Boudin, Corot, and Courbet. High prices and an atmosphere unfortunately lacking in warmth.

Hostellerie du Moulin du Pré. 14860 Bavent (near Cabourg). Tel. 31 78 83 68. An inexpensive, whitewashed inn built on the site of an old cider mill. Excellent *prix-fixe* meals.

Hostellerie du Moulin du Vey. 14570 Le Vey par Clécy (in the Suisse Normande). Tel. 31 69 71 08. A 200-year-old mill in a romantic, dreamlike setting on the Orne River. Modestly priced, somewhat dowdy rooms and good food in the timbered, barnlike dining room.

Hotel Normandy. 14800 Deauville. Tel. 31 88 09 21. A lavish turn-of-the-century hotel overlooking the boardwalk and the sea, with gracious Norman courtyards, red clay tennis courts, and an atmosphere both refined and chic.

Verte Campagne. 50660 Trelly (northeast of Avranches). Tel. 33 47 65 33. A delightful find—a small, 16th-century farmhouse with eight plain, very reasonable rooms and wonderful food for the price in a tiny, stone-walled dining room with a massive period fireplace.

WHAT TO SEE

Normandy is rich in natural and historic sights and intriguing museums. For visiting the province in depth, the Michelin green guide to Normandy is indispensable, as is a fine-grain map of the region. We found that the very smallest roads—usually the "white" roads on most maps, many beginning with the letter D, such as the D27 just inland from the coast west of Deauville —yielded the most beautiful landscapes. We recommend, where time permits, that you travel from point A to point B on these tiny back roads.

Among the sights we would urge you not to miss are:
- The Landing Beaches from Arromanches to Le Hoc Point
- The Abbaye of Le Bec-Hellouin
- The Bayeux Tapestry and the Museum Baron-Gérard
- The Town of Villedieu-les-Poêles and the copperware ateliers and bell foundry
- The town of Honfleur with the Église Sainte-Catherine and the Musée du Vieux Honfleur and the Musée Eugène Boudin

- Rouen, particularly the Place du Vieux Marché and the rue du Gros-Horloge, the Fine Arts Museum with its wonderful collection of Rouen faience, and of course the magnificent Notre-Dame Cathedral
- The primeval region of the Suisse Normande
- The *belle époque* boardwalk and town of Cabourg, made famous by Proust
- The Haras-le-Pin stud farm
- The drive along the "Normandy Corniche" from Trouville to Honfleur on the D513 road
- The "Nez de Jobourg," a spectacular promontory reached after a half-hour walk from the end of the D202 road, south of Goury at the tip of the Manche.

WHERE TO EAT

Bayeux Le Lion d'Or, 71 rue St.-Jean.
Tel. 31 92 06 90.

Beaumont-en-Auge L'Auberge de l'Abbaye.
Tel. 31 64 82 31.

Bénouville (about six miles northeast of Caen) Manoir d'Hastings.
Tel. 31 93 30 89.

Beuvron-en-Auge Le Pavé d'Auge, Place du Village.
Tel. 31 79 26 71.

Carentan L'Auberge Normande, 17 boulevard de Verdun.
Tel. 33 42 02 99.

Cherbourg Le Vauban, 22 quai de Coligny.
Tel. 33 53 12 29.

Deauville Ciro's, on the boardwalk.
Tel. 31 88 22 62.
Le Kraal, place du Marché.
Tel. 31 88 30 58.
Le Yearling, 38 avenue Hocquart-de-Turtot.
Tel. 31 88 33 37.

Dieppe La Bucherie (about two miles outside of town on the DN27 in Les Vertus).
Tel. 35 84 24 26.
Marmite Dieppoise, 8 rue St.-Jean.
Tel. 35 84 24 26.

Dives-sur-Mer (near Cabourg) Guillaume le Conquérant, 2 rue d'Hastings.
Tel. 31 91 07 26.

Honfleur L'Absinthe, 10 quai de la Quarantaine.
Tel. 31 89 39 00.
L'Ancrage, 12 rue Montpensier.
Tel. 31 89 00 70.

Pierrefitte-en-Auge Les Deux Tonneaux.
Tel. 31 64 09 31.

Pont l'Évêque L'Auberge de la Touques, Place de L'Église.
Tel. 31 64 01 69.

Rouen Bernard Warin, 9 rue Pie.
Tel. 35 89 26 69.
Beffroy, 15 rue Beffroy.
Tel. 35 71 55 27.
Dufour, 67 rue St.-Nicolas.
Tel. 35 71 55 27.

Trouville Brasserie les Vapeurs, 160 quai F. Moureaux.
Tel. 31 88 15 24.

ICI MOULES Spéciales prêtes à la cuisine

INDEX

Both Pierre LeVec and Pierre Moulin have vivid memories of Normandy during World War II. As a member of the 82nd Airborne Division of the United States Army, Pierre LeVec participated in the D-Day invasion of June 1944. As a teenager Pierre Moulin was sent from Paris to safety on a farm in Normandy, where he spent several years of the war. Even for those of us born after the war, the experience of visiting Normandy's battlefields and cemeteries is extremely moving. For these reasons, our heartfelt gratitude goes to the valiant ones who gave their lives in the Battle of Normandy to preserve beauty and freedom for all of us.

—*L.D.*